RACE AND RACISM

Ruth Benedict

RACE AND RACISM

LONDON

ROUTLEDGE & KEGAN PAUL LTD

BROADWAY HOUSE: 68-74 CARTER LANE, E.C.

First published in England 1942
Second impression 1943
Third impression 1945
Fourth impression 1951
Fifth impression 1959

Printed in Great Britain by
Lowe and Brydone (Printers) Limited, London, N.W.10

CONTENTS

CONTENTS

FOREWORD

I SUPPOSE every anthropologist has had the same experience. When his lecture is over and he has shown that racism has no scientific basis for its claims of congenital superiority for any one race or nation, some listener gets to his feet and says, "But the Negroes"—or the Japanese, or the Indians—"are *not* Whites." Then the anthropologist, who has probably spent years of his life patiently investigating racial differences, has to say again that to recognize Race does not mean to recognize Racism. Race is a matter for careful scientific study; Racism is an unproved assumption of the biological and perpetual superiority of one human group over another. The confusion between race and racism is not confined to the man on the street. Whenever scientists issue a statement contradicting the racist claims of some Chamber of Commerce campaigning against recent immigrants in America, some university professor will write and say, "But races differ, and I know it." Then the weary anthropologist is tempted to answer him, "On the point you raise, consult for confirmation the last thirty titles of my bibliography." For it is no paradox that a student may have at his tongue's end a hundred racial differences and still be no racist.

Confusion between the facts of race and the claims of racism is almost universal in the modern world, and this volume is arranged to show that they are poles apart. They are different in their history, in their votaries, in the data they make use of. I have put together in the

vii

first section of the book what is scientifically known about Race; in the second part I have reviewed the history of Racism. In the final chapter I have written an anthropologist's answer to the questions: "Why is there an epidemic of racism in the world today?" and "How could we stop the epidemic?"

In writing this book I am indebted to all who have worked on the subject of race and especially to the greatest of living anthropologists, Professor Franz Boas, who has read this book in manuscript. My reason for writing it is twofold. I believe that those of us who are members of the vaunted races and descendants of the American Revolution should make it clear that we do not want or claim the kind of superiority the racists offer us. I believe that those of us who are anthropologists should expose the travesty of sober anthropological material which racism offers.

RUTH BENEDICT.

PART I : RACE

Racism : The *ism* of the Modern World

As EARLY AS the late 1880's a French pro-Aryan, Vacher de Lapouge, wrote: "I am convinced that in the next century millions will cut each other's throats because of 1 or 2 degrees more or less of cephalic index." On the surface it appears a fantastic reason for world wars, and it was certainly a reason new under the sun. Was he right? What could it mean? The cephalic index is the quotient of the greatest breadth of the head divided by its length, and some tribes and peoples over the world run to high indices and some to low. Narrow heads are found among uncivilized primitives and among powerful and cultivated Western Europeans; broad heads are too. Neither the narrow heads of the whole world nor the broad heads stack up to show any obvious monopoly of glorious destiny or any corner on ability or virtue. Even in any one European nation or in America men of achievement have been some of them narrow-headed and some broad-headed. What could it mean that "millions will cut each other's throats" because of the shape of the top of their skulls?

In the long history of the world men have given many reasons for killing each other in war: envy of another people's good bottom land or of their herds, ambition of chiefs and kings, different religious beliefs, high spirits, revenge. But in all these wars the skulls of the victims on both sides were generally too similar to be distinguished. Nor had the war leaders incited their followers against their enemies by referring to the shapes of their heads. They might call them the heathen, the barbarians, the

B

heretics, the slayers of women and children, but never our enemy Cephalic Index 82.

It was left for high European civilization to advance such a reason for war and persecution and to invoke it in practice. In other words, racism is a creation of our own time. It is a new way of separating the sheep from the goats. The old parable in the New Testament separated mankind as individuals: on the one hand those who had done good, and on the other those who had done evil. The new way divides them by hereditary bodily characteristics—shape of the head, skin colour, nose form, hair texture, colour of the eyes—and those who have certain hallmarks are known by these signs to be weaklings and incapable of civilization, and those with the opposite are the hope of the world. Racism is the new Calvinism which asserts that one group has the stigmata of superiority and the other has those of inferiority. According to racism we know our enemies, not by their aggressions against us, not by their creed or language, not even by their possessing wealth we want to take, but by noting their hereditary anatomy. For the leopard cannot change his spots and by these you know he is a leopard.

For the individual, therefore, racism means that damnation or salvation in this world is determined at conception; an individual's good life cannot tip the balance in his favour and he cannot live a bad life if his physical type is the right sort. By virtue of birth alone each member of the "race" is high caste and rightly claims his place in the sun at the expense of men of other "races." He need not base his pride upon personal achievement nor upon virtue; he was born high caste.

From this postulate racism makes also an assertion about race: that the "good" anatomical hallmarks are the monopoly of a pure race which has always throughout history manifested its glorious destiny. The racialists

have rewritten history to provide the scion of such a race
with a long and glamorous group ancestry as gratifying
as an individual coat of arms, and they assure him that
the strength and vigour of his race are immutable and
guaranteed by the laws of Nature. He must, however,
guard this pure blood from contamination by that of
lesser breeds, lest degeneration follow and his race lose
its supremacy. All over the world for the last generation
this doctrine has been invoked in every possible kind of
conflict: sometimes national, between peoples as racially
similar as the French and Germans; sometimes across
the colour line, as in Western fears of the Yellow Peril;
sometimes in class conflicts, as in France; sometimes in
conflicts between immigrants who arrived a little earlier
and those who came a little later, as in America. It has
become a bedlam.

Where all people claim to be tallest, not all can be
right. In this matter of races, can the sciences to which
they all appeal judge among the babel of contradictory
claims and award the decision? Or is it a matter of
false premises and bastard science? It is essential, if we
are to live in this modern world, that we should understand Racism and be able to judge its arguments. We
must know the facts first of Race, and then of this doctrine
that has made use of them. For Racism is an *ism* to
which everyone in the world today is exposed; for or
against, we must take sides. And the history of the future
will differ according to the decision which we make.

WHAT THEY SAY

In this there is nothing new: that when a philosopher
cannot account for anything in any other manner, he
boldly ascribes it to an occult quality in some race.

Walter Bagehot, *Physics and Politics*. London, George
Routledge & Sons Ltd.

The white race [today read *Nordics*] originally possessed the monopoly of beauty, intelligence, and strength. By its union with other varieties [read *Alpines, Mediterraneans*] hybrids were created, which were beautiful without strength, strong without intelligence, or if intelligent, both weak and ugly.

> Arthur de Gobineau, *Essay on the Inequality of Human Races.* Translated by Adrian Collins. London, William Heinemann, 1915, p. 209.

List of physical characteristics of the genuine Teuton:

The great radiant heavenly eyes, the golden hair, the gigantic stature, the symmetrical muscular development, the lengthened skull (which an ever-active brain, tortured by longing, had changed from the round lines of animal contentedness and extended towards the front), the lofty countenance, required by an elevated spiritual life as the seat of its expression.

> Houston Stewart Chamberlain, *The Foundations of the Nineteenth Century.* London, John Lane, 1910, Vol. I.

What racists say of their own race:

Judgment, truthfulness, and energy always distinguish the Nordic man. He feels a strong urge toward truth and justice. . . . Passion in the usual meaning of the rousing of the senses or the heightening of the sexual life has little meaning for him. . . . He is never without a certain knightliness.

> Hans F. K. Gunther, *The Racial Elements of European History.* Translated from the second German edition by G. C. Wheeler. London, Methuen & Co., 1927, pp. 51, 52.

In mental gifts the Nordic race marches in the van of mankind.

> Baur, Fischer and Lenz, *Human Heredity.* Translated by Eden and Cedar Paul. London, Allen & Unwin, 1931, p. 655.

What racists say of other groups:

Many intellectuals are trying to help the Jews with the ancient phrase, "The Jew is also a man." Yes, he is a man, but what sort of a man? The flea is also an animal!

Goebbels, reported in *Time*, July 8, 1935, p. 21.

If non-Nordics are more closely allied to monkeys and apes than to Nordics, why is it possible for them to mate with Nordics and not with apes? The answer is this: it has not been proved that non-Nordics cannot mate with apes.

Herman Gauch, *New Foundations for Research into Social Race Problems*. Berlin, 1933. Cited by J. Gunther, *The Nation*, February 5, 1935.

People who live in glass houses:

Opinions about our ancestors

FIRST CENTURY B.C.: Do not obtain your slaves from Britain because they are so stupid and so utterly incapable of being taught that they are not fit to form a part of the household of Athens.

Cicero to Atticus.

ELEVENTH CENTURY: Races north of the Pyrenees are of cold temperament and never reach maturity; they are of great stature and of a white colour. But they lack all sharpness of wit and penetration of intellect.

Saïd of Toledo (a Moorish savant), quoted in Lancelot Thomas Hogben, *Genetic Principles in Medicine and Social Service*. London, Williams & Norgate, 1931, p. 213.

Race : What It Is Not

CHINESE HAVE a yellowish skin and slanting eyes. Negroes have a dark skin and wide flat noses. Caucasians have a lighter skin and high thin noses. The colour and texture of the hair of these peoples differ as much as do their skin and noses. These are outward and visible signs by which we recognize race; they are racial characteristics. In briefest possible definition, race is a classification based on traits which are hereditary. Therefore when we talk about race we are talking about (1) hereditary and (2) traits transmitted by heredity which characterize all the members of a related group. The first necessity in discussing race is to outline what race is *not*. A great deal of the confusion about race comes from confusing hereditary traits with traits which are socially acquired.

In the first place, race and language are not the same. This should be obvious, for not all who speak Arab are Arabians and not all who speak English are of the White race. Nevertheless the confusion occurs constantly.

A man's hereditary features and the language he speaks depend upon two different sets of circumstances. His hereditary anatomy depends upon his remote ancestors, and his language depends upon the speech he heard when he was a child. From the point of view of human morphology these two are not even related, for whatever the inherited conformation of his oral cavity and vocal cords, a child learns to speak any language spoken about him, and children with the same oral conformation speak languages with the most different sounds. If not even a man's speech organs account for the language he speaks, still less do racial features like skin colour, cephalic index, eyes, and hair determine his mother tongue. The Negroes in America speak English or Spanish or Portuguese or French, depending upon the language of the country in which they live; and Negroes without White blood speak languages as readily as the light-brown. According to their associations they speak with the intonations of the poor White of the area or of the privileged minority. And this is not a situation which is new in the world. So the primitive Manchus who came from the Siberian tundras have for centuries spoken in China a pure Chinese, and the Arab language was spread after the ninth century over immense areas of northern Africa among peoples of Negroid blood.

When the people of one race speak the same language and that language is spoken only by that one race, as among some primitive tribes, this is not because the two are interdependent but because they both depend on a third circumstance. This circumstance under which both physical form and language take shape and become unique is isolation. In prehistoric times the world was sparsely populated, and in isolated regions both physical type and language might become different from those in any other part of the world. The process is so simple that it is the more remarkable that it did not happen oftener than it did. The principal reason why it did not was that isolation was so often broken. When two peoples became thoroughly intermingled by conquest or inter-marriage, their descendants were racially one mixed type; but they spoke one or the other language.

There was also another factor which operated in history from the earliest times. Racial types maintain themselves over longer periods and over greater areas than language does; people of the same racial type commonly speak several languages which cannot be reduced to a common linguistic family. In the early history of mankind this must have been even truer than it is today, for widespread languages, like Bantu and Polynesian, were once restricted to small groups and have spread far and wide only in comparatively recent times; in parts of the world like the Caucasus and like aboriginal California the early condition still survives. Languages in these latter areas stop short at the margins of one valley, but the racial type is the same over great areas. From earliest times, therefore, language and race have had different histories and different distributions; in the modern world they are shuffled like suits in a pack of cards.

In spite, however, of the impossibility of arguing from race to language or from language to race, race and language are constantly confused. *Aryan*, the term now used in Germany for the preferred race, is the name of a group of languages which includes the Sanskrit of ancient India and languages of ancient Persia; and *Aryan* has also been commonly used as a term covering a much larger group of languages, the Indo-European, which includes not only Sanskrit and Old Persian but German, English, Latin, Greek, Armenian, and Slavic. In whichever sense *Aryan* is used, it is a language term and has no reference to a peculiar German racial heritage. Because of the ludicrous inapplicability of the first sense of the word *Aryan*, the Nazis, when they selected the term, were obviously thinking of it in the latter sense of *Indo-European*. But the people speaking Indo-European languages have no unity of racial type either in skin, in eye or hair colour, in cephalic index or in stature.

The foremost student of the Aryan languages in the last century, Max Müller, exposed the fallacy vigorously even in the 1880's—a fallacy which had already become current through the writings of Thomas Carlyle, the English historian J. R. Green, and the French racialist

Count de Gobineau. "I have declared again and again," Max Müller writes, "that when I say Aryas (Aryans) I mean neither blood nor bones nor hair nor skull; I mean simply those who spoke an Aryan language. When I speak of them I commit myself to no anatomical characteristics. To me an ethnologist who speaks of Aryan race, Aryan blood, Aryan eyes and hair, is as great a sinner as a linguist who speaks of a dolichocephalic [narrow-headed] dictionary or a brachycephalic [broad-headed] grammar." [1] Nevertheless, as we shall see in discussing the history of racism in Europe, the list of sinners has increased rather than diminished since Max Müller's time. [2]

The fundamental reason why language cannot be equated with race is that language is learned behaviour, and race is a classification based on hereditary traits. Language is only one special instance of how learned behaviour varies in mankind without relation to physical type. It was not only the Chinese language that the Manchus learned in China; they took over Chinese architecture, the forms of Chinese family life, Chinese ethics, Chinese literature, Chinese food. It is not only the English language that American Negroes use; they become Baptists and Methodists and Pullman car porters. Instead of learning, as in Africa, the elaborate technicalities of "throwing the bones" for divination, they learn the technicalities of reading and writing; instead of the complexities of *mankala*, the intricate peg-game of Africa and the Near East, they learn to shoot craps. Their culture becomes American.

For culture is the sociological term for learned behaviour: behaviour which in man is not given at birth,

[1] *Biography of Words and the Home of the Aryans.* London, 1888, p. 120.
[2] I have myself in this volume used *Slav*, which refers to languages, as a racial term. There is no word in popular usage which designates this group in biological terms.

which is not determined by his germ cells as is the behaviour of wasps or the social ants, but must be learned anew from grown people by each new generation. The degree to which human achievements are dependent on this kind of learned behaviour is man's great claim to superiority over all the rest of creation; he has been properly called "the culture-bearing animal." He does not grow wings or fins to cross the seas; he builds ships and airplanes, and the building and operating of these are culturally transmitted. He does not grow fangs and claws to kill his enemy; he invents gunpowder and Maxim guns. This non-biological transmission is a great advantage in that it allows for much greater adaptability to circumstances, but it progressively lessens the importance of biologically transmitted behaviour.

This elementary truth is essential for the understanding of race. Race is biologically transmitted, and among the social insects and to a lesser degree among the carnivores their tastes in food, their ways of obtaining it, their aggressiveness or lack of aggressiveness in assuring their own survival are also biologically transmitted. That "the leopard cannot change his spots" means that the leopard, because he belongs to a certain species, will always be found stalking the jungle for his prey. But in man the great aggressors of yesterday become the mild peace-lovers of today. In the ninth century Scandinavians were the feared aggressive Vikings of the sea; in the present generation they are the peaceful non-aggressive exponents of co-operatives and the "middle way."

Even more commonly, at the present time the non-aggressors of yesterday become the aggressors; their race has not changed, but their behaviour has. Japan has a history of peace and non-aggression that cannot be matched in the Western World. During the first eleven centuries of her recorded history she was engaged in only one war abroad. Indeed this sole conflict ended in 1598, and from that time until 1853, when Japan opened her doors to intercourse with the world outside, the building of all ocean-going boats was forbidden by imperial decree to make certain that Japan would preserve her policy of isolationism. The ceremoniousness, the light-heartedness, the aesthetic appreciation of the Japanese were traits that passed current as their essential qualities. Since 1853 they have fought five times overseas and are well on their way to becoming one of the most aggressively warlike nations of the world. In the human race no centuries-long existence free from conflict as the lamb's guarantees that the next generation may not become the lion.

There is another aspect of this fact that race and culture are distinct. In world history, those who have helped to build the same culture are not necessarily of one race, and those of the same race have not all participated in one culture. In scientific language, culture is not a function of race.

The more we know about the fortunes and the vicissitudes of any civilization, the less it proves to be the peculiar offspring of an unmixed race. This is true even far back in prehistory, and an eminent archaeologist has said that the great social truth made clear by archaeology is that culture lives on and maintains itself though the race perish; either as conquerors or as peaceable settlers a new racial type carries on the old ways of life of the conquered or earlier occupants of the land. The archaeologist looking back over the long centuries sees, not the destruction of that civilization when one racial carrier was superseded, but the continuity of its history in the hands of one racial type after another. The growth of human civilization in the European Palaeolithic (Old

Stone) Age has cultural, but not racial, continuity. The
culture which Neanderthal Man possessed was after his
disappearance carried forward by Cro-Magnon man,
given new embellishments by men of the later Old Stone
Age, and elaborated by the races of the New Stone Age.
Only the last two types are racially ancestral to modern
man. This lack of racial continuity in the small corner
of Europe during prehistory is better established for
Europe than for other parts of the world because the
archaeology of Europe is better known, but all that prehistoric research is uncovering in Africa, in Asia, and in
Central America tells the same story.

This story has been repeated in Western civilization
since the dawn of history, and the evidence of it constantly
accumulates. A century ago the historian of Western
civilization was content to begin with Greece, but today
this is inadequate. Historical study has unrolled a longer
history under our eyes. Greece was the inheritor of
earlier Oriental civilizations and its early culture owed
much to Egyptian influences. Essential cornerstones of
our civilization are the inventions of other races. Perhaps
we describe this civilization of ours as built on steel and
gunpowder. But steel was invented either in India or
in Turkestan, and gunpowder in China. Perhaps we
prefer to identify our Western culture by its printing
presses and literateness. But paper and printing were
both borrowed from China. Our economic life with its
great concentration of population is based on the cultiva-
tion of grains and of animals which are Neolithic inventions from Asia; corn and tobacco were first domesticated
by the American Indian. Our control of nature is overwhelmingly dependent on mathematical calculations.
But the so-called Arabic system of notation which is
essential to all complicated mathematics was unknown
in Europe in the Roman era; it was invented in Asia

and introduced to our civilization by the Moors. Algebra was a method of calculation also borrowed by Europeans from Asiatic peoples.

Wherever we look, the truth is forced upon us that many different races have contributed to the growth of our culture, and that when we hold culture as the constant, race is a variable. The White race was once the borrower as today Japan is. The White race spent long centuries at the process and Japan a few decades, but by that token some literalists could argue the racial superiority of the Japanese over the White race.

When we look at the fact of cultural-racial separateness from the other side, this time holding race constant, we find that the culture of any one race is of many degrees of complexity. While certain groups of a given race forge ahead and set up great states or build great cities which are architectural triumphs or carry out great public works, other groups of the same race may remain primitive nomadic herdsmen. A race does not move forward as a whole. So some groups of Arabs built up great states under Sultans with regal splendour, the arts and sciences flourished, and they were in the vanguard of the civilization of their day. Other members of the same race were simple Bedouins following their herds from pasturage to pasturage. Similarly the primitive Amur River tribes of Siberia or the Yukaghir of the Siberian tundras are of the same race as the civilized Chinese. The Malay race also has its half-wild primitive tribes of the coastal Malay Peninsula and at the same time its centres of high civilization. Race is not a touchstone by which civilized people can be separated from uncivilized. Rude people of barbarian ancestry have shown themselves to be abundantly able to adopt the highest extant civilizations and to contribute to their development.

The Manchus were a rude and unnoted nomadic Tungu tribe, but first through contact with the Mongols, and later by their conquest of China in the mid-seventeenth century, they became the ruling dynasty of a country unsurpassed in riches and glory at that period. Wherever we look—to the Malays, the Manchus, the Mongols, the Arabs, or the Nordics—the same story repeats itself over and over.

The Nordics belong to this list, and no one need quarrel with the extravagant claims that have been made for their "manifest destiny" if these same claims are allowed also for all other rude peoples who have come to participate ably in the building of civilization. When, however, the Nordics are singled out as a peculiar instance and their participation in civilization credited to their racial type and not to the universal processes of history, it is easy to recognize the special pleading. It is closer to actual history to speak of them as Hooton does—as "the rawboned ruffians from the North," [1] whose irruptions shattered the peace of early Europe—or to call attention, as Hankins [2] does, to the fact that they "destroyed civilizations more frequently than they created them." The point to note, however, is that they were a group with certain inherited features, and that though they were once rude, they later became exponents of a great civilization; their former rudeness in no way disqualified them from participating ably in its development.

History cannot be written as if it belonged to one race alone. Civilization has been gradually built up, now out of the contributions of one race, now of another. When all civilization is ascribed to the "Nordics," the claim is the same one which any anthropologist can hear

[1] Hooton, Earnest A., *Up from the Ape.* London, Allen & Unwin, 1931, p. 525.

[2] Hankins, Frank H., *Racial Basis of Civilization.* New York, 1926, p. 350 ; London, Knopf, 1927.

any day from primitive tribes—only they tell the story of themselves. They too believe that all that is important in the world begins and ends with them; the creator gave to them exclusively in the beginning all that is good and at their downfall will destroy the world. We smile when such claims are made by a rude and tiny American Indian tribe or a naked Papuan of New Guinea, but ridicule might just as well be turned against ourselves. After all, the world of these tribes extends but a little way beyond their borders and folk-tales serve them for history; their exaggerated claims are the result of ignorance. But when the same crude provincialism is put forward learnedly in our day, it is still a childish primitive error maintained in the face of all that historians have ascertained and in the face of modern knowledge of the whole extent of the globe.

Provincialism may rewrite history and play up only the achievements of the historian's own group, but it remains provincialism; it is not history. The lesson of history is that pre-eminence in cultural achievement has passed from one race to another, from one continent to another; it has embraced not whole "races" but certain fragments of an ethnic group which were for certain historical reasons favourably situated at the moment. Peace had been achieved for a certain period, or freedom from exploitation for certain groups. All those of the race who were within the range of these conditions profited by them, and the arts of life were advanced; individuals of whatever race rose to the opportunity and have often left their names enrolled in history. It has happened in Mesopotamia, in China, in India, in Egypt, in Greece, in Rome, and in England. Obviously no racial type has a monopoly of high culture.

It behooves us, therefore, to study race historically and biologically and anthropometrically without expecting race to account for all human achievements. Race is a scientific field of study. But human history is a vastly more complicated thing than a mere record of the distribution of anthropomorphic measurements, and cultural achievements are not mechanically transmitted and guaranteed by any racial inheritance.

WHAT THEY SAY

Since biological change occurs slowly and cultural changes occur in every generation, it is futile to try to explain the fleeting phenomena of culture by a racial constant. We can often explain them—in terms of contact with other peoples, of individual genius, of geography—but not by *racial* differences.

> R. H. Lowie, *An Introduction to Cultural Anthropology.*
> New York, Farrar & Rinehart, 1934, p. 9. This
> author's *Are we Civilized?* London, George Routledge
> & Sons Ltd., 1929.

The growth and spread of civilization has gone on with a serene indifference to racial lines. All groups who have had an opportunity to acquire civilization have not only acquired it but also added to its content. Conversely, no group has been able to develop a rich or complex culture when it was isolated from outside contacts.

> Ralph Linton, *The Study of Man.* London, D. Appleton-
> Century, 1936, p. 54.

If we can once thoroughly convince ourselves that race, in its only intelligible, that is, biological, sense, is supremely indifferent to the history of languages and cultures, that these are no more directly explainable on the score of race than on the laws of physics and chemistry, we shall have gained a viewpoint that allows a certain interest to such mystic slogans as Slavophilism, Anglo-Saxondom, Teutonism, and the Latin genius, but quite refuses to be taken in by any of them.

> Edward Sapir, *Language.* New York, Harcourt, Brace & Co., 1921, pp. 222-223.

The Role of Nordics in History.

The racists say

It is only shameful indolence of thought, or disgraceful historical falsehood, that can fail to see in the entrance of the Germanic tribes into the history of the world the rescuing of agonizing humanity from the clutches of the everlastingly bestial.

> Houston Stewart Chamberlain, *The Foundations of the Nineteenth Century.* Translated by John Lees. London, John Lane, 1910, Vol. I, p. 495.

The historians say

The material culture of the Nordics was not originally superior to that of the Danubian peasants or the megalith-builders; in Transylvania they appear frankly as wreckers; in the ancient East and the Aegean they appropriated and for a time impaired older and higher civilizations.

> V. Gordon Childe, *The Aryans.* London, Kegan Paul, 1926, p. 207.

Even in a political and military sense no convincing case can be made for Nordic supremacy during the medieval period.

> H. E. Barnes and H. David, *The History of Western Civilization.* New York, Harcourt, Brace & Co., 1935, Vol. I, p. 446.

They do not like each other's languages.

French

The native or acquired difficulty among the Germans of getting the nervous centres of the *medulla oblongata* to carry out the orders of the cerebral centres regarding syllabic sound-production—they say *fa* and *pa* for *va* and *ba*—is a pathological fact still observable in our own day.

> Honoré Joseph Chavée, *Bulletin Sociale Anthropologie*, 1873, p. 505, quoted by Jacques Barzun in *Race, A Study in Modern Superstition*. London, Methuen & Co., 1938.

German

The Nordic race alone can emit sounds of untroubled clearness whereas among non-Nordic men and races the pronunciation is impure, the individual sounds confused and more like noises made by animals.

> Herman Gauch, *New Foundations for Research into Social Race Problems*. Berlin, 1933, p. 165.

Summary.

The so-called racial explanation of differences in human performance and achievement is either an ineptitude or a fraud.

> Arnold Joseph Toynbee, *A Study of History*. London, Oxford University Press, 1934, Vol. I, p. 245.

THREE

Man's Efforts to Classify Himself

IN ALL MODERN SCIENCE there is no field where authorities differ more than in the classifications of human races. Some have separated races on the basis of geographical distribution, some on the basis of skin colour, some on the basis of cephalic index, some on a combination of several traits. Some have divided mankind into three races, some into seventeen, some into thirty-four. Some have made primary an ethnic group which another authority has made secondary. This lack of agreement is not a matter of scientific perversity but is due to the facts of human history and the known principles of biology—two subjects which we shall discuss in the following chapters. But first it is necessary to consider the material on which any classification of human races must be based and the categories that are in use.

Racial classification of the human species has an honourable background. Similar classification in botany and zoology has progressed from the crude eighteenth-century categories of Buffon to the more basic ones, established in modern use, which group living forms to show genetic relationships and to indicate evolutionary sequence.

The scientist has before him the results that have been attained in the study of living forms other than human, and he knows the pitfalls of superficial resemblances. In zoology a classification is considered artificial if, for instance, it classes a whale with fishes simply because whales swim; the classification is basic when it classes a whale with mammals, whose processes of reproduction and need for breathing air into their lungs the whale

shares. For the study of mammals, it is necessary to
subordinate many obvious physical differences that
appear among mammals, and to consider together not
only whales, which swim like fishes, but also bats, which
fly like birds. Whales and bats, moreover, must be
studied alongside hoofed animals and men, for they are
all mammals.

Students of human races, therefore, hoped to establish
classifications of man which were more than superficially
descriptive and which might have a validity such as the
classification of mammals has.

Before the time of Darwin the basis for such classification was fundamentally different from that used today.
In those days the question at issue was polygenesis (many
origins) versus monogenesis (one origin). The position
stated in the Bible and accepted by the Church was that
all men were sprung from Adam, and this position was
traditional in pre-Columbian Europe. The voyages of
discovery, however, and the widening of the world under
man's eyes made another possibility attractive, for how
was one to account for yellow men and black men and
red men without a number of special acts of creation?
We must remember that in those days nobody knew how
widely the yellow race varied within itself, or the black
race, or the red; nor was it known how these groups
shaded off one into another. The races were seen as a
series of contrasted pictures like those in our own
elementary geographies.

There were monogenists who believed that climate had
produced these varieties of mankind. Among these the
most famous was the Baron de Montesquieu, whose *Spirit
of Laws* was published in 1748. There were also the poly-
genists who believed that these varieties were separate
"thoughts of God" and unrelated one to another.
Geoffroy St. Hilaire in the French Academy in 1830

argued against the monogenist Cuvier, who derived all races from Noah through his three sons, Ham, Shem, and Japheth, and Goethe's excitement over this debate shows well the place this controversy had in contemporary thought. "What do you think of the great event?" he exclaimed to a friend of his. "The volcano has broken out, everything is in flames, and it's no longer something going on behind closed doors. You cannot imagine what I felt on hearing the news of the meeting." [1]

Even before Darwin there were learned students who challenged this idea that each race was a separate entity. The first great anthropologist, Theodor Waitz, argued against it on the basis of physical measurements of different races. He showed that racial stereotypes failed to correspond to the facts : the Yellow Man or the Red Man included whole series of types, some of them more like Europeans, for instance, than they were like other groups of their own race. Waitz wrote without knowledge of Darwinism, though his *Anthropology* was published in the same year as the *Origin of Species*, and we must therefore not credit Darwinism alone with dealing the death-blow to this old controversy. Nevertheless Darwin's idea of species and the interpretation he gave to the anatomical similarities between man and the higher apes deprived the controversy of any point. It threw the whole argument into a wider context, and in this context all the primates, including all races of man, became branches of one family tree.

Since Darwin, all racial studies have had a different background from the earlier controversies. They accept the family tree to which all mankind belongs and attempt to determine in how far human varieties have biological significance.

[1] *Gespräche mit Eckermann*, III, p. 240, quoted by Jacques Barzun in *Race, A Study in Modern Superstition*. London, Methuen & Co., 1938, p. 63.

It was immediately evident that mankind did not include a series of fully developed species, the proper criterion for which was, according to Darwin, sterility or the production of sterile offspring if they were crossed. Nothing was more obvious than the fact that fertile children were born from the mating of even the most extreme types of the White race with the most extreme types of Negro or Mongolian; intermixture of different ethnic groups had occurred constantly in history and was occurring at an increasing rate as men became more mobile in a world where transportation facilities were more ample.

The idea of species, however, underlay all the thinking of the period, and if human varieties could not be separated one from another by mutual sterility, the criteria must be found in some physical characteristics. To serve as racial criteria these characteristics must be present in the whole race in some fashion peculiar to that race alone: as, for example, extremely dark pigmentation, frizzy hair, and a certain form of broad, flat nose are found nowhere but among Negroes. A whole range of characteristics have been studied and used as racial criteria in this sense, and the results of these studies are necessary for a modern understanding of race.

Skin Colour.

The racial difference that at once arrests attention is skin colour. The wall paintings of ancient Egyptians used four pigments for the complexions of the four peoples they knew: red for themselves, yellow for their enemies in Asia, white for people from the north, and black for Negroes. This classification has been reduced by one and given a Greek terminology. Its value consists in that it is the most generalized category into which human beings are zoologically divided:

> Leucodermi—white-skinned;
> Xanthodermi—yellow-skinned;
> Melanodermi—black-skinned.

In general usage this classification corresponds to the division into Caucasoid (white), Mongoloid (yellow), and Negroid (black); these are the obvious and striking human varieties. Further physical characteristics, as we shall see, can be associated with these three groups. They have each a large geographical range, and represent real differentiations.

Skin colour of itself, however, has very limited scientific use as a criterion of these primary races. The range in each group is very large and some groups of Whites are darker than some Negroes. Broca, the French physical anthropologist, used thirty-four shades of skin colour and Deniker nine. Differentiation into shades is a help in one direction but it makes the overlapping even more serious.

The superficial character of skin colour as a criterion of race becomes a serious difficulty when the question is one of assigning problematic groups to the primary races. Are the Australians Negroid because their skin colour is nearest the range for Negroes? Are light-coloured Armenian types Caucasoid because theirs is nearest the range for Whites? All students agree that such arguments are superficial.

Skin colour, therefore, as a means of differentiating the ethnic groups of man with the widest geographical range has some advantage if it is loosely applied. As a scientific criterion it has a gross rather than a specific usefulness.

Eye Colour and Eye Form.

Eye pigmentation is commonly recorded in physical measurements of populations but it does not identify an

individual as a member of a particular race. Dark eyes
are common to all human races and cannot therefore be
used to differentiate them. Even more special types of
eye colour, such as blueness, have never been found co-
extensive with a whole ethnic group.

Eye form appears in racial descriptions primarily in
reference to the "slanting" eyes typical of yellow-skinned
Asiatics. It is called the Mongoloid eye, and the slant-
eye appearance is caused by a fold of skin, the epicanthic
fold, which covers the inner angle of the eye. It occurs
in infancy among many Whites but does not usually
persist into adulthood; it occurs among some Negroes
and is characteristic of some American Indians (also
Mongoloids), though most of these latter do not have it.

Hair Colour and Hair Form.

Dark hair colour, like dark eyes, is so widely distributed among mankind that it does not serve to define
race, and, as with blue eyes, even the special trait of
blond hair does not run uniformly through any ethnic
group.

Hair form can also be classified. There are three major
types:

> Leiotrichy—straight lank hair (e.g. Chinese, Eskimo);
> Cymotrichy—wavy hair (e.g. inhabitants of Europe,
>   India, Australia);
> Ulotrichy—woolly or frizzy hair (e.g. Negroes,
>   Melanesians).

These differences in hair appearance are due to the form
of the individual hair as seen in cross-section under a
microscope: straight hair is round, woolly hair extremely
oval, and wavy hair falls in between.

Again, like skin colour, these different hair forms are
found in ethnic groups of wide geographical distribution,

and when used as characteristics of these major groups they have descriptive value. The trouble with them as racial traits is that they cross-cut races as described in other terms. Because Australian blackfellows have smooth wavy hair, like that of Europeans, they are not therefore Europeans, nor are the Eskimos Chinese because they have straight lank hair. Smooth wavy hair is typical of Europe, Egypt, and the Asiatic peoples who live from the eastern Mediterranean down to and including India, and is therefore characteristic of peoples who are unlike in other physical traits. Hair form nevertheless has a certain value in the study of the distribution of races, and no one doubts, on other grounds as well as hair form, that the dark Melanesians of western Oceania—for instance, the natives of the Solomon Islands—are genetically related to African Negroes.

Shape of the Nose.

Physical anthropologists have paid considerable attention to measuring the types of human nose. There are two chief categories:

Leptorrhine—narrow nostrils (e.g. European, Eskimo);

Platyrrhine—flat broad nostrils (e.g. Negroes, Tasmanians).

Besides these, various descriptions of the nose bridge are in use: concave, convex, aquiline, or straight.

Here, again, though certain extreme nose shapes are found only in certain groups in the world—certain broad, flat forms among certain Negroes and certain narrow aquiline ones among certain Caucasians—even these do not identify a man who on other counts is a Negro or a Caucasian, both races having a great range of nose shapes.

Stature.

Bodily height is the extreme case of a physical trait which, though it is also hereditary, is easily modified by environment. Many studies have demonstrated that stature as well as body weight is influenced by diet, sickness, and other conditions of life. It is therefore in most cases not a reliable index of genetic relationship. A good exception to this rule is the case of the pygmies, among whom stature is clearly hereditary and can be used for zoological classification. In other cases, however, even when stature is hereditary, tall groups jostle short groups within each race as it is defined in other terms. The tallest and the shortest group measured are both Negro, and even on the remote island of Tierra del Fuego, an extremely tall American Indian tribe is the neighbour of an extremely short tribe. Stature is a very fallible racial criterion.

Cephalic Index.

The cephalic index is the ratio of the maximum breadth to the maximum length of the head seen from on top, and is expressed in a percentage. This aspect of the head has been arbitrarily divided into three types:

Dolichocephalic—narrow - headed, with cephalic index under 75;

Mesocephalic—medium - headed, with cephalic index 75-80;

Brachycephalic—broad-headed, with cephalic index over 80.

Of all human measurements, the cephalic index is the commonest in physical anthropology and the data on it in a given population are the most often available. This is because it is definite and easy to measure, and because, with certain allowances for the thickness of the skin, it can be used in measurements of skulls as well as of heads of living people.

The cephalic index does not serve to distinguish the White race from the Mongoloid nor from the Negro, nor has it any constant value for any primary race. For instance, some American Indian groups have the narrowest skulls ever measured and some the broadest skulls; and these are groups which, judged by other characteristics, fall together into one race. Similarly, the cephalic index distinguishes between certain sub-groups of the White race rather than having a constant value for all Caucasians. In other words, a graph of the cephalic index shows peaks and valleys *within* large groups otherwise similar and is chiefly used to describe small local variations.

These are the most important anatomical features which have been used as racial traits. There is also, in a somewhat different field, the study of blood groups. Knowledge of blood groups arose from experience in the transfusion of blood, when it was found that the blood from certain persons was fatal to some others. It was discovered that at least four blood types could be differentiated, and this held out high hopes to students of races. The technique of determining the blood type is simple, and the very first work on races showed that one blood group was concentrated among Asiatic Mongoloids, another in Western Europe, and a third among American Indians and Eskimos, who are Mongoloid in the usual classification.

Blood types are strictly hereditary and very stable; any individual having a blood type A, for example, must have had one or both parents whose blood type was A. Therefore when different blood types are present in any

population, it is one of the surest signs of mixed ancestry.
But even such isolated races as the aboriginal Australians
have a high percentage of blood group A, which is that
most characteristic of Western Europe. And high percentages of blood group B, that most characteristic of
India and Eastern Asia, are found throughout Europe.
The evidence from the study of blood groups emphasizes
in the strongest possible manner the great amount of
biological mixture that must have taken place from the
earliest times.

We are now prepared to understand some of the
problems that have increasingly faced those students of
human races who have attempted to establish biologically
valid categories of mankind. No one doubts that the
groups called Caucasoid, Mongoloid, and Negroid each
represent a long history of anatomical specialization in
different areas of the world; but great numbers of individuals cannot be assigned to one or another of these
races on the basis even of several of the above criteria.
There are Whites who are darker than some Negroids;
dark hair and eyes are common among all races; the
same cephalic index is found in groups of the most diverse
races; similar hair form is found among ethnic groups
as distinct as native Australians and Western Europeans;
blood groups do not define races.

Racial differentiation might, nevertheless, depend upon
certain combinations of these anatomical characteristics.
But these traits are not co-extensive. If a student takes
skin colour first, he will have in Sweden, for instance, a
considerable number of fair-skinned individuals. If he
adds fair hair and blue eyes to this first category, he will
have to cut down his group numerically. He may then
add tall stature and again rule out many individuals.
By adding narrow-headedness he eliminates certain

others. He has now a tall, blond-haired, blue-eyed, fair-skinned, narrow-headed group. But it is a series of individuals, not the population of Sweden. Retzius, who measured thousands of army recruits in Sweden, a country which is famous for the combination of characteristics we have just enumerated, found that only 11 per cent. conformed to this description, and this in spite of the fact that three of his criteria—fair-skinned, blue-eyed, and blond-haired—are all aspects of one type of pigmentation and might be expected to occur together. If he had added other anatomical criteria his group would have been smaller yet.

In order to understand the significance of such a situation, let us imagine that a zoologist listed five traits which distinguished a variety of black bears. He then measured the group which of all groups in the world was most characterized by these traits and found that only 11 per cent. conformed. He would certainly decide one of two things: either he had chosen traits which were too variable within the group to be definitive, or the group was the result of mixture with other varieties, and could not serve as an original type.

In exactly similar fashion the physical anthropologist has to consider these two possibilities. The traits he has selected may have been suggested merely from his own superficial experience and not be the ones which characterize Sweden. Since, as we have seen, dark hair, dark eyes, and not-fair skin are characteristic of the human race as a whole, the opposite traits of blond hair, blue eyes, and fair skin which occur in Sweden arrest his attention. Extreme features always stand out unduly, whatever they are. But this susceptibility of his to blondness, which caused him to set up his criteria in this way, was obviously not a function of the actual composition of the Swedish population but of the strangeness of blond features in comparison with the darker colouring of other human groups. It was a shot in the dark which was not borne out by measurements.

On the other hand, the physical anthropologist has to consider a second possibility: his 11 per cent. who are tall, fair, blue-eyed, yellow-haired, narrow-headed may represent an original pure type which has been attenuated by intermarriage and "swamped" by other immigrants, but it may still be a true representative of a pure original race. In this case the physical anthropologist has to square his interpretation with the biological laws of heredity; specifically he has to take account of the facts technically known as the independence of segregation: that is, how inherited items from both ancestral lines, whether hair colour or intelligence, split up in any such intermingling of blood and get sorted out in new combinations in the offspring. (See pp. 54-58.) Inheritance always works in this way. Hence, once mingling has occurred, no individual samples can represent the original race *in toto*, even though there are living individuals in whose veins its blood still runs.

Whether the physical anthropologist measures Swedes or Algerians or Chinese or Greeks, the same difficulty presents itself. Over and over again he discovers the obvious consequences of the great intermixture that has occurred, or he discovers that the universality of the "ideal" type he set out to investigate in a given group is an illusion. If he compares his findings in his own group with those of another investigator in a different group—comparing, for example, Swedes with Sicilians—he finds that none of his traits are utterly lacking in individuals of the other group. The statistical distribution is different; that is all. He set out to isolate an anatomical variety of mankind as he would isolate a species of birds, but the facts he has gathered prove only that the human situation does not correspond to the situation among birds.

The physical anthropologist, therefore, has no recourse but to give up the parallel with birds and dogs, and to work out some classifications which correspond to the facts he has accumulated. When he does this, he has to say: In great areas of the world certain anatomical specializations have occurred in mankind and of these the most definite are the Caucasoid, Mongoloid, and Negroid. In exactly the same manner, but to lesser degree, specialization has occurred also in more restricted areas, but showing in many respects, as in that of the cephalic index, numerous identical forms in all primary races. These anatomical specializations are old and were clearly marked at the dawn of history; high cultural development, however, is recent and appears now in one area of the world, now in another. It does not follow the fortunes of any one of these races, whether we use the term in the sense of the three major stocks or in the sense of small subdivisions of these. (See pp. 91-93.) The present distribution of bodily form in the world can be understood only by virtue of our historical know-ledge of the migrations of peoples from the earliest Palaeolithic to the present day (Chapter Four), and this disproves the existence of "pure races" in any centre of Western civilization.

We are left, therefore, with the task of describing, first, the major human stocks, and then an indeterminate number of local specializations. In the major stocks the characteristics are, of course, quite generalized since they must overspan so many local variations within the stock.

The Caucasian is relatively hairy, has smooth (wavy to curly) hair, minimum prognathism (jaws projecting beyond the plane of the face), a fairly high, thin nose, and straight eyes. (N.B.—Caucasians have no characteristic cephalic index or body height, no specific hair colour or eye colour; their noses may be Roman or concave; even the colour of their skin is extremely variable.)

Mongoloids have very little facial and body hair, and their head hair is lank and straight. (N.B.—Skin colour varies too widely to admit of definition; the slant eye is local and among American Indians is absent except sporadically; cephalic index covers the whole known human range; nose form also runs from Roman to concave.)

The Negroid type has the darkest skin range: kinky hair, thick lips, frequent prognathism, a flat nose. (N.B. —The body height of Negroes is extremely variable, including the tallest and shortest groups known, and their cephalic index is also variable though narrow-headedness is general.)

Boas has suggested that it is ethnically more correct to reduce even these three primary stocks to two, the Mongoloid and the Negroid, and to place the Caucasic type as a local specialization of the Mongoloid. He points out that this would do least violence to the facts in accounting for the Caucasic traits of the Ainu, an aboriginal group of Japan. All observers have commented upon the likeness of the Ainu to the White race, not only in skin colour but in their hairiness, which is the trait that sets them most conspicuously apart from the surrounding Mongoloids. If this type represented by the Ainu and the Whites were potential among Mongoloids, the likeness of Ainu and Whites would represent two conspicuous parallel developments without having to be accounted for by a hypothetical migration.

Before the dislocations following the discovery of the New World, the three present-day major stocks were each distributed around a major body of water: the Caucasians around the Mediterranean, the Negroids around the Indian Ocean, and the Mongolians around the Pacific. Specifically Negroid peoples are characteristic not only of Africa but of the Western Pacific, the Oceanic Negroids being called Melanesians, literally "black islanders." The Mongoloids were distributed not only in Asia but through the length and breadth of the New World, those of the New World being the American Indians.

It is clear also that no scientific purpose is served by speculating about the allocation of doubtful peoples to one or another primary stock. It only happens that Caucasian, Mongoloid, and Negro have the widest distribution in the world and the most definite anatomical traits. "Three" is not a sacred number which rules that the history of these three stocks is older than, or different from, other groups now marginal. As more physical characteristics are considered, more and more groups have to be differentiated. The Australian aborigines, or even the Bushman-Hottentots, may be representative of now marginal groups which were once widely distributed over the world. On the other hand, the Polynesians may be a well-marked variant due to racial crossing at some remote period. If human zoology pointed to an original fixed series of pure races, it would be important to get an answer to these questions; since, however, all evidence points in the direction of progressive and local variations upon one human theme, these questions become bio-logically of little importance.

These progressive and local specializations in physical traits occurred not only in the primary races and in other distinctive races, like the Polynesian and Australian; they occurred also within each widespread race, differentiating sub-groups, now in regard to cephalic index, now in regard to height or hair colour or complexion. In the most commonly used classifications based on anthropo-

C

morphic measurements, the Caucasians of Europe fall into three subdivisions: Nordic, Alpine, and Mediterranean. The Nordics, in Northern Europe, have frequent blond pigmentation, tall stature, and narrow-headedness. Nordics are found in Russia, Finland, Estonia, Lithuania, Scandinavia, Holland, Belgium, Germany, France, and England. The Alpines, in Central Europe, have variable body build, usually stocky, medium pigmentation, and broad-headedness. They are predominant in Germany and France and extend into the central highlands of Europe and as far east as eastern Rumania. The Mediterraneans, in Southern Europe west of the Adriatic, have light body build, somewhat darker pigmentation, and the narrow-headedness of the Nordic. These distributions refer to concentrations only, for the populations of Europe all include significant numbers of individuals who conform to types whose concentration is in another area. Nevertheless, the distribution of cephalic index measurements, for instance, is marked. These distributions of physical type run roughly horizontal across the European map; they do not differentiate present nations of Europe like Germany and France, which both include a northern strip in which the Nordic type occurs and a much wider strip in which Alpines predominate.

The Mediterranean and the Alpine types both include many peoples outside of Europe.

The Alpine sub-group extends, in Asia as well as in Europe, through a belt north of the Mediterranean peoples. They are therefore sometimes called Eurasiatics. In the words of an authority who has most recently written on European physical anthropology, Carleton Coon: "The geographical extent of the Alpine racial type is enormous, reaching from France to China. Throughout this extent it maintains a nearly constant form, in stature, in the dimensions of the head and face, in pilosity, and in general morphological features." [1]

The Mediterranean sub-race includes the Hamites, who form the bulk of the population of Egypt, and the Semites, so called from the language they speak. The Bedouins of Arabia are, in Coon's phrase, "of pure Mediterranean race," [2] and the same authority places in this group Irano - Afghans of Persia and Afghanistan.

The lack of any correlation between race and sovereign states is obvious. The individuals who plan the policies of Germany or France or who shout together in the streets over a national victory in war are united not by the similarities of their cephalic indices or by any common family tree, but by the fact that they read the same newspapers and will be called upon to die for the same flag. An Alpine individual of Germany will not feel mystic kinship and common cause with the fierce Georgians of the Caucasus or the Tajiks of Russian Turkestan though they all belong to one branch of the human family tree, nor will an Italian Mediterranean with a Bedouin. Both Alpine and Mediterranean sub-groups form majorities in communities of vastly different cultural complexity, and, unless indoctrinated by racialists, they do not split up into warring parties on the basis of different physical types.

The actual distribution of physical types in the world, and especially in Europe, cannot be understood without some review of historical migrations and conquests and intermingling of peoples, and to such facts we must turn in the next chapter.

---

[1] Coon, Carleton, *The Races of Europe*. London, Macmillan & Co., 1939, p. 646.
[2] *Ibid.*, p. 623.

WHAT THEY SAY

Races as irreducible categories exist only as fictions in our brains.

Jean Finot, *Race Prejudice*. Translated by Florence Wade-Evans. London, Constable & Co., 1906, p. 317.

The different races of man are not distinguished from each other by strongly marked, uniform, and permanent distinctions, as are the species belonging to any given tribe of animals. All the diversities which exist are variable, and pass into each other by insensible gradations.

J. C. Prichard, *Natural History of Man*. London, H. Baillière, 1855, p. 473.

The bones of a stunted Nordic are almost indistinguishable from those of an overgrown and muscular Mediterranean. The Nordic is supposed to have a longer and narrower face, larger brow ridges, and a more sloping forehead, a longer, narrower and higher nose, and a more boldly jutting chin. But I do not believe that any physical anthropologist can with certainty distinguish the skeletal remains of the taller individuals of the Arab sub-race of Mediterraneans from those of a Nordic.

E. A. Hooton, *Up from the Ape*. London, Allen & Unwin, 1931, p. 526.

FOUR

Migration and the Mingling of Peoples

MIGRATION IS AS OLD as mankind. Somewhere in the Old World our arboreal ancestors gradually reached the human level and man began his first and most spectacular migration. Neanderthal Man seems to us now a defenceless, apelike creature, but he had at least fire and stone tools. During the early Glacial Periods he spread from Asia into Europe and occupied a great part of it. But Neanderthal's migrations were as nothing compared to those of the early forms of Homo Sapiens which followed him. Gradually but irresistibly, by the beginning of historic time, man had occupied the whole round earth. He had not accepted Land's End barriers, but had pushed into the New World in the region of Bering Strait and had occupied the continents of the Americas from Alaska to Tierra del Fuego. With the simplest savage equipment—no boats, no agriculture, no breeding of animals—he even reached Australia and maintained himself in its punishing deserts.

No other animal form has so spectacular a history, no other has established itself under so many environmental extremes. It would be reasonable to suppose that defenceless early man, in accommodating himself to a damp equatorial forest or to a barren arctic tundra, would have grown himself a different body, that his organs would have assumed different forms; in other words, that he would have differentiated into species, as the deer family is represented by the reindeer and the elk in the sub-arctic and by different varieties of true deer in the temperate and tropical zones. The marvel is that man's physical form remained stable, and that, instead, he was able to survive under all these difficult conditions by virtue of his inventions : ways of building houses, ways of clothing himself, ways of procuring food. His one physical adjustment which may have survival value is skin colour; dark pigment has been shown to act as a filter against the actinic rays of the sun, which in large quantities are harmful to man. Specialization in dark pigmentation therefore would be an advantage to tropical people. The other human specializations, like differences in the shape of the skull, lank or curly hair, even short or tall stature, do not in themselves show any survival value and seem from this point of view almost irrelevancies.

From another standpoint these specializations, however, are anything but irrelevancies. Man is much more interested in himself and his varieties than he is in any other series of facts, and differences which pass unregarded when they hold between various breeds of mice are, between various breeds of man, the occasion of persecution and deportation. Nevertheless, from the zoological standpoint they remain surprisingly small and arbitrary.

To understand the map of physical differences we have to turn to the facts of history. The dramatic spread of mankind over the whole world had two aspects: first, that of man's gradual infiltration into all parts of the world; and second, that of his localization and isolation in relatively permanent occupation of certain areas. Man, that is, was not only spectacularly mobile, but he also settled down. The world during the Stone Age was sparsely populated, and a group that established itself in one territory might remain in occupation of it for centuries. During all that time no alien peoples might press upon them; the group might breed and die for generations, a world unto itself. Whether the total group which made up this "world" was large or small, this meant inbreeding, and under primitive conditions the group was often very small indeed. No two people in the tribe, under such conditions, could marry without having whole series of ancestors in common, and therefore anatomical traits which seldom appeared elsewhere might by this inbreeding even become the rule. Curious specializations occur. The Lapps have a ridge along the middle line of the palate, and the Inca of Peru specialized in an interparietal bone in the skull. These are anatomical minutiae which arose originally by mutation (see p. 60) and have been made common in these corners of the world by inbreeding of family lines.

Such an area, where a settled inbreeding group becomes differentiated from other groups in secondary characteristics, has been called "an area of characterization." [1] Thus Eastern Asia was an area of characterization for the slanting eye, and a great region extending from India to Western Europe an area for smooth wavy hair. Under very early human conditions, when the tempo of migration was much slower than it is today, people in some areas of characterization bred together for so many centuries that they must have approached racial purity. Geneticists count that with the strictest inbreeding for some seventeen generations—which would mean today the continuous inbreeding of some strain since before Columbus was born—they can get a strain which satisfies genetic requirements of purity; it would breed true. To get this strain in the laboratory they cross only descendants of one pair and are satisfied with nothing less. Such inbreeding must always have been rare in human societies, but there may well have been an approximation to it in some undisturbed areas, and these conditions, however they fell short of ideal requirements, favoured diversification of bodily form among the human race.

[1] Haddon, A. C., *Wanderings of Peoples*. London, 1912, p. 47.

But areas of characterization occur in exactly similar fashion after such groups have interbred one with another. Permanence of occupation was always being disturbed either by climatic changes or by pressure of other tribes, and when this occurred and two hitherto isolated groups came into contact, we know from the physical measurements of their descendants that they mixed. It used to be thought that at least Homo Sapiens had not mixed with Homo Neanderthalis, his more ape-like predecessor in Europe. But intermediate skeletons have been unearthed which are believed to show that even these most divergent of known human forms inter-bred, and some students have now identified traces of Neanderthal inheritance in modern European races. Certainly all racial types since that time have interbred whenever they came together in the same region. The countries of such inbreeding became areas of char-acterization. Gradually, out of the hereditary traits contributed by the component groups, a group arose which differed from all these ancestors, but had certain stable anatomical traits.

The world today still has areas of characterization in which new human types have only recently been stabilized. Several such areas have been studied and they are indubitable, for we know the parent races that went into the mixture and the length of time it has taken to produce the new stable variety. Such a modern in-stance, to be comparable to earlier ones, must be an area where the offspring of racially distinct parents have interbred. The necessary isolation may be geographic, as on Pitcairn Island, where descendants of six English sailors, the mutineers of the famous *Bounty*, and of the Tahitian (Polynesian) women who accompanied them in their desperate escape from civilization have lived and been inbreeding since 1790. Oftener the isolation is social and the mixed bloods come to form an intermarrying group distinct from the native community or that of the Whites. This has happened among the Bastaards in South Africa, where descendants of Boers and native Hottentot women have maintained themselves as an in-breeding group and in the course of several generations have developed a stable type which differs from that of either ancestral group. The same thing is happening today among the Anglo-Indian groups in India, even in great urban centres.

The first and essential step toward understanding race in the world today is the recognition of the fact that these areas of characterization are unlimited in number. There certainly existed in earlier times many areas of characterization, the representatives of which are not found today, though their "blood" is now inextricably mingled in various degrees in surviving races. It is impossible to reconstruct their original physical type. Their skeletons have perished, or, even if some are extant, many traits used in racial differentiation are irretrievably lost. From certain other areas of characterization, hordes spread out and established themselves over two continents; under favourable conditions they multiplied, bred with the previous occupants of distant parts, and formed new areas of characterization.

Within the area of characterization, we must remember, there had to be a certain permanence of occupation and inbreeding. The situation is so different in urban centres of Western civilization today that we are usually unaware of its implications. These vast concentrations, drawn from every corner of the earth, and their members ready to move on to new pastures tomorrow, are new to human history. They do not give the conditions under which racial types readily become fixed. Such conditions are represented, rather, by the peasant population of much of Europe—people rooted in the land they cultivate, and inbreeding within narrow confines. Our cities might become areas of specialization if national and international machinery broke down and every man's life were safe only within the walls of Berlin or London; if this persisted for generations their heterogeneous populations of the moment would, in course of time, become homogeneous, that is, something that would warrant the name of a stable race.

An understanding of the distribution of racial types in the world is possible only against this background of multiple centres of characterization in which certain hereditary traits become fixed, only to mingle with those from some other area, and again to become stabilized in a new type after mixture, and then to repeat the cycle. At best, all the physical measurements of all the people in areas of true inbreeding throughout the world give us only the distribution of contemporary areas of characterization; they will not identify for us a few primary races from which all subsequent races have been derived by straight descent or by intermixture. We must accept human history for what it is, and try to think not in terms of a few primary races but in terms of an indefinite number of areas of characterization. As we have seen, most such areas have come about through recombinations of traits drawn from some mingling of former stabilized types. "Man," says the biologist Julian Huxley, "is unique among species of animals in the degree to which crossing between already differentiated groups and types has taken place. Accordingly, multiple ancestry is at least as important as common ancestry in considering the nature and origins of any group." [1]

Though multiple ancestry played a rôle of great im-

[1] Huxley, Julian, and Haddon, A. C., *We Europeans*. London, Jonathan Cape, 1935, p. 95.

portance in the history of old and stable racial types, it is even more apparent in modern Europe and America, where pressure of population in old communities has, owing to better transportation facilities and sometimes to political or religious conditions, resulted in an unparalleled mobility of populations. But the essential process is not new; it has been going on for centuries. Before we talk glibly about the common ancestry of Germans or Frenchmen or Old Americans, we must recognize the omnipresence of this multiple ancestry brought about by centuries of migration.

Voltaire once read a book which began: "The Franks from whom we Frenchmen are descended." "Hello, my friend," he wrote, "who told you so?" The Franks, one minor detachment of the Teutonic "barbarians" who overran Gaul in the sixth century A.D., contributed their quota to the multiple ancestry of France, as well as of Germany, but, though they gave France their name, they were only one sub-group of the Teutonic peoples who, although at the time they seemed to "destroy civilization," were absorbed into its population. The Franks are one minor incident in the long history of the movements of peoples which have affected the ancestry of France. In Old Stone Age times the land was occupied by a people whose drift had been across southern Asia, northern Africa, into Spain, and finally into France. In New Stone Age times several branches of the Mediterranean race and early Alpines came from the east, and by the seventh century B.C. Celtic invasions disturbed the earlier settlers. By the first century B.C. it was the Belgae and the Cimbri from Denmark who were the spearheads of barbarian invasion, and though this was checked for a long interval by the expansion of the Roman Empire, by the first century A.D. the Vandals had overrun Gaul and the Visigoths established a kingdom in the south of France which lasted through the seventh century A.D. It was in the fifth century, which saw the "fall" of Rome, that the Franks overran much of France, the Goths erupted into the southern provinces, and the Huns swept into Gaul under Attila.

Out of all this succession of different peoples from different areas of characterization certain local types have developed in different regions of modern France. It is even possible that the early Palaeolithic inhabitants of the country have left their mark in the bodily form found in southern provinces such as Dordogne and the cantons of the Pyrenees. The Mediterranean coast is characterized by short, dark, narrow-headed peoples— the Mediterranean sub-race. The mountains of Savoy and of Brittany and a great central belt of France are predominantly Alpine, and in some parts of south-central France the broad-headedness is extreme. In Normandy to the north, especially near the mouth of the Seine, there is a certain concentration of blond, narrow-headed people (Nordic). None of these types is peculiar to France alone, and in no region is any one of these types exclusive. The only groups who deserve the name of a stable race are inbred, long-settled peasants in remote valleys of the Rhone.

The composite racial history of France is not exceptional in Europe. It is from certain points of view less extreme than that of Germany, for in eastern Germany we have to take account of the Slavs, whose area of characterization seems to have been somewhere east of Poland. In the first few centuries of our era the Slavs occupied the whole of the present eastern Germany, and though a backward wash of German colonists later established the German language in this region, the population remained predominantly Slavic in physical type. "Eastern Germany is in many places more Slavic than Russia."

Nor is Europe exceptional in its history of migrations and racial mixtures. The story in Asia and Africa is the same, and if in post-Columbian America and in European colonies it seems to us to have become extreme, this is at least partly because we see with our own eyes, instead of having to be told by history, the mixture of racial types. But fundamentally it is still the same old story. If a motion-picture film could condense into a half-hour's spectacle the hither-and-thither journeyings of mankind in the Old World, Americans would recognize in the mixture of peoples in the nations of Europe the very thing we have seen happening in Pennsylvania or in Minnesota. Just as the Pennsylvania Dutch (Germans) or the Minnesota Swedes are today gradually losing their separatism and intermarrying with once-alien groups, so the Celts, the Latins, the Slavs, and the Nordics have mingled. Just as in America there are still concentrations of blonds or of big noses in certain places, so in Europe there are certain concentrations of types. But in America the process is so obvious that we recognize how absurd it would be to measure all the cephalic indices of California and compare them, as a unit, with the cephalic indices of Ohio, or to compare the pigmentation in Illinois with that in Pennsylvania. We recognize that such counting could have no biological meaning. But the German "race" and the French "race" rest on the same absurd foundation, and are just as meaningless biologically.

In Europe, just as in America, the "blood" of peoples occupying the same territory mixes, and their offspring inherit from both sides. This process has not in the past caused civilization to stop short in its tracks. It is useless to frame arguments about either its good or its bad effects, for since it is universal in human history, neither human advancement nor human disaster can be chalked up to this cause. Obviously, because of historic conditions, which had nothing specifically to do with the "mixture of blood," the consequences of migration and conquest have been sometimes "good," sometimes "bad," according to the point of view of the period at which account is taken. All the rest is special pleading.

Nothing illustrates this special pleading more clearly than the famous attempts to explain the fall of Rome. The Romans themselves attributed it to the inroads of barbarians who overran and swamped the great Empire which had so noble a history. They did not analyse their own weaknesses and mistakes of the two centuries that had gone before the fall; the catastrophe was due to the barbarians. This view served the Renaissance, too. Deeply committed to classical views, the Renaissance was able to add that the destruction of classical civilization by the Vandals had thrust Europe into eight centuries of the Dark Ages. *Vandalism* became a vernacular word for wanton destruction of everything fine and precious. Europeans of a later date, proud of their descent from these Teutonic hordes, offered a different interpretation. The Teutons had saved Europe from "the everlasting bestial"; they were young human gods who cleared the world of an effete race. But, these spokesmen of Teutonic racism pointed out, the fall of Rome contains a lesson for us today: Rome fell because she mingled her "blood" with that of the barbarians. Had she passed laws forbidding mixture, she would have prevented her own destruction. Thus the fall of Rome came to be for Teutonic racists a moral tale that proved the necessity of racial hygiene.

History tells the tale otherwise. Rome in the fourth and fifth centuries, passing laws of racial hygiene to stop the march of history, would have been like King

Canute commanding the tides to stop short. The Emperors could not by such acts have legislated away the declining vigour of the Roman administration of the world and the loss of leadership she had suffered. Internal developments in the Roman Empire had weakened it, and the Teutonic hordes took advantage of this weakness; a few centuries earlier they had been powerless against its strength. The decline of the Roman Empire is a long and complex story of lack of vision and of internal violence. At last she was no longer mistress of the world. While she was vigorous, she Romanized whole areas of alien peoples; intermixture accompanied her great period as well as her decline. Racist explanations of the fall of Rome are a travesty of the facts.

The exaggerated claims that are made for programmes of racial hygiene are, therefore, not upheld by historical evidence. Nevertheless, patriots in most of the Western nations have warned their fellow-citizens of the evils of racial intermixture with some lesser breed. In America we are told that the Nordics must save themselves pure from contamination with peoples of Southern Europe. In Germany racial purity is not lost by marriage with a Japanese, but defilement comes from marriage with a Jew. The English in India regard intermixture as betrayal of White supremacy. The evils of these prohibited mixtures in Germany and in India are unquestioned; they are apparent to any observer. Those who have themselves made mixed marriages and the children of such unions are the first to testify to the unsatisfactory situation in which they find themselves.

Modern instances of the evils of racial mixture do not, however, prove that intermixture is a biological evil. In the first place, history has shown that such mixed races have flourished and progressed even in those extreme cases where intermixture has been across the colour line. The Arabs are of Caucasian race, and have always taken wives freely from among the native peoples. In their dispersement over Northern Africa a mixed race of Black and White grew up which created great kingdoms of wealth and splendour. In the western Sudan these kingdoms culminated in the sixteenth century in the great Empire of Bornu. Moslems have never attached importance to ancestry, and there was no adverse discrimination against the offspring of Arabs and the native women of their harems. On the contrary, intermixture produced great political leaders and men of wealth, and facilitated the spread of higher culture.

Even in some parts of the modern world mixture of races shows no evil effects. Students have always pointed this out for Hawaii, where the code of racial separatism has been conspicuously lacking. Intermixture in Hawaii does not have to be illicit; marriages between the most diverse races take place in the churches. There is no discrimination against the offspring of such crosses; they can hold eminent positions if they have ability. At the governor's receptions and university dances there is no colour line. The cultural development of Hawaii has not suffered.[1]

When, therefore, we find in many parts of the world glaring evidence of the mediocrity of the half-caste, it is worth examining the social discrimination to which he is subjected. Where there is strong racist sentiment, the Eurasian or the Eurafrican is an outcaste among both the kin of his father and the kin of his mother. His mother is scantily provided for, and when he is grown he must confine himself to inferior jobs allotted to his kind. The cards are stacked against him. Social discriminations of this kind prevail generally in the world today, and most

---

[1] Adams, Romanzo, " The Unorthodox Race Doctrine of Hawaii," in *Race and Culture Contacts*, ed. by E. B. Reuter. New York, 1934, p. 145 ff.

objective observers say frankly that not many of the dominant "race" would, if they lived under similar conditions, make a much better showing. Some Whites, though born to poverty and brought up as outcastes, would nevertheless rise to positions of eminence. But so also do some of the half-castes.

The social rather than biological explanation of the low condition of mixed bloods in most parts of the world is borne out by anthropometric studies. "Hybrid vigour" has been shown in studies of American Indian-White mixture, stature in the half-breeds being greater than that of either race contributing to the cross. Mixed bloods also show over and over again evidence of increased fertility. The descendants of the famous English-Tahitian cross on Pitcairn Island had during their early life on the island one of the highest rates of increase yet recorded. Nature apparently does not condemn the half-caste to physiological inferiority.

The rule for the breeding of good human stock is that both parents be of good physique and good mental ability. Since the best quarter of the world's population according to these standards includes individuals of all races, on the basis of any measurements yet devised, improvement of human stock is not a matter of racial separatism. "Good" ancestry has been given a racist meaning in the modern world and may include progenitors that are very inferior when reckoned by standards either of health or of mental ability. As is well known, individual offspring rise even above such a handicap. It is, however, a handicap which has to be reckoned with, whatever the social conditions. Half-castes, when they have healthy and capable ancestors, have never been shown to be similarly handicapped by nature. "If," says Julian Huxley, "the alleged inferiority of half-castes really exists, it is much more likely to be the product of the unfavourable social atmosphere in which they grow up than due to any effect, which would be biologically very unusual, of their mixed heredity." [1]

The movements of peoples over the face of the earth, therefore, inevitably produce race mixture and have produced it since before history began. No one has been able to adduce evidence of its inherent evil. It has sometimes been a social advantage, sometimes a running sore threatening the health of the whole society. It can obviously be made a social evil, and, where it is so, sensible people will avoid contributing to it and grieve if their children make such alliances. We must live in the world as it is. But the evil of racial intermixture has no known basis in the immutable laws of nature. The doctrines of racism have much to answer for, but the lot of the half-caste in the world today is one of the bitterest fruits they have produced.

WHAT THEY SAY

Thus from a mixture of all kinds began
That heterogeneous thing, an Englishman.

Daniel Defoe, *The True-Born Englishman.*

Every civilized group of which we have record has been a hybrid group, a fact which disposes effectually of the theory that hybrid peoples are inferior to pure-bred ones.

Ralph Linton, *The Study of Man.* London, D. Appleton-Century, 1936, p. 34.

There is no necessity to postulate the existence of a specific and universal instinct of racial antipathy; while

[1] Huxley, J. S., *Eugenics and Society :* Galton Lecture, Eugenics Society. London, 1936.

on the other hand there is strong positive evidence that such an instinct does not exist. An adequate explanation of racial antagonisms can be found in impulses and motives that are independent of race.

These impulses and motives, however, though not racial in their origins, may become racial, through being connected in the mind with the thought of another race. When this association takes place the feelings may be aroused by contact with any member of that race, and operate with all the force of an instinctive antipathy.

> J. H. Oldham, *Christianity and the Race Problem.* London, S.C.M., 1924, p. 43.

The racist says:

This accurately expresses the racial view held by National Socialists [i.e. the Third Reich in Germany]: that each race on this earth represents an idea in the mind of God. This is just what we do believe, and therefore we call for a clear-cut differentiation between blood and blood, so that God's idea may not be blurred and caricatured in the half-breed.

> W. Gross in *Racio-Political Foreign Correspondence,* published by the Bureau for Human Betterment and Eugenics. Berlin, April 1935.

But the biologist says:

The sociologist who is satisfied with human society as now constituted may reasonably decry race crossing. But let him do so on social grounds only. He will wait in vain, if he waits to see mixed races vanish from any biological unfitness.

> W. E. Castle, " Biological and Social Consequences of Race-Crossing." *American Journal of Physical Anthropology,* Vol. IX, p. 156.

And the Brazilian statesman says:

In South America our experience of centuries has taught us that there is no real understanding except the one that comes through the fusion of races.

Dr. Oliviera Lima, quoted by Cedric Dover in *Half-Caste*. London, Secker & Warburg, 1937, p. 248.

FIVE

What is Hereditary?

HEREDITY IS the transmission of traits from parents to offspring. An "old American's" heredity comes to him from his biological ancestors, as any other Anglo-Saxon's comes to him from his biological ancestors; their ancestors may have something in common but much that is diverse. They are not the same persons, and their heredity will therefore not be the same. For one to speak of his "Aryan," Anglo-Saxon, or Jewish heredity is biologically meaningless, for it lumps together as one's ancestors vast numbers of people who are in no sense one's forebears, and does not distinguish all those varied human types who are actually one's ancestors. If mankind were a series of mutually infertile species, such as those into which wild animals are divided, this lumping would not be a serious error; no family line of the red deer has ancestors who were elk; all of them were exclusively red deer. As we have seen, however, human beings do not fall biologically into species of this kind; differentiated human types cross and recross, and the only ancestry that accounts for the individual is his own. Heredity in this sense follows very precise biological laws, many of which are known, but racial heredity in Western Civilization is a myth which sets up, in place of true heredity in family lines, an absurd picture of heredity from a race. *Race* is an abstraction even as it is defined by a geneticist; as it is defined statistically by a physical anthropologist it is even more of an abstraction. It is not the *race* which copulates and reproduces.

Heredity from parent to child is studied in the science

of genetics. Though its foundation was laid in Darwin's *Origin of Species*, which was published in 1859, modern genetics is based on Mendel's studies of garden peas— work which was done shortly after the publication of the *Origin of Species* but remained unknown until 1900. The facts which Mendel observed contradicted in several ways the expectations of Darwinian evolutionists. These earlier evolutionists had expected to find that heredity operated to produce a uniform blend, as if the heritable traits of the mother and those of the father were respectively a trickle of ink and a trickle of water which mingled in their offspring to form a uniform watered ink. But this is an over-simplification. The rôle of bisexual reproduction proves, as the result of Mendelian observation, to be much more complex than this. Inheritance is passed along to the offspring as a long series of characteristics contributed by the father and the mother, and these have to be conceived not as ink and water mingling but as a pile of beads sorted out anew for every individual. For many traits these sortings follow certain statistical rules. Mendel in his studies of garden peas followed out the process in detail, and since there are many biological problems in human heredity that remain to be solved, it is still necessary to describe the process from observations of plants and animals.

Mendel riveted his attention upon the history of tallness or dwarfness, yellowness or greenness, in generations of peas, that is, upon a single pair of alternative characters at a time. He crossed a tall pea with a dwarf pea and got all tall peas. He then allowed this generation of peas to cross-fertilize itself and the picture changed: though three-quarters were tall, one-quarter of all the resultant pea plants were dwarf and bred true to dwarfness as if their ancestors had never been crossed with a tall variety. Long series of experiments showed that tallness and dwarfness—like yellowness and greenness, smoothness and wrinkledness—sorted themselves out in offspring but retained their identity; in biological terms each is an *allelomorphic pair* and represents alternative characteristics of a single trait. For most traits one of these alternatives is *dominant* over the other; that is, the non-dominant, or *recessive*, trait will not be visible in the offspring even though it can be transmitted to the next generation. The original male parent peas had a double dose of the dominant factor (or gene) for tallness (TT) and the original female pea a double dose of the recessive trait for dwarfness (dd). Since tallness was dominant, the first generation (F^1) were all tall, having, each of them, a single dose of tallness and a single dose of dwarfness (Td), of which the dwarfness did not show. But dwarfness was not lost. The next inbred generation (F^2) inherited Td from *both* parents, and, just as when you make all possible combinations of two long matches and two short matches, the unit characteristics in this generation were in the proportions of: TT, Td, dT, dd.

Diagram I

Female Parent, F^1

		TALL	dwarf
Male	TALL	F^2: TALL TALL	F^2: dwarf TALL
Parent, F^1	dwarf	F^2: TALL dwarf	F^2: dwarf dwarf

Since T was dominant, the first three groups all had the same appearance, that of TT. That was why Mendel's peas in the F^2 generation were one-quarter dwarf and three-quarters tall.

The importance of this law of inheritance is that it laid

the basis for understanding the rôle of sexual reproduction in giving rise to new combinations of traits. Mendel went on to see what happened when parents differed, not in one allelomorphic pair but in two. He bred tall (T) yellow (Y) peas with dwarf (d) green (g) peas, yellow being dominant over green, as tallness is over dwarfness. The problem was to find out whether dwarfness always stayed with greenness and tallness with yellowness. But he found that in F^2 the numerical distribution in the offspring was independent of the original "type" the parent generation represented; the unit characteristics could, again, be sorted out like different matches or different beads. Since two allelomorphic pairs are involved, the distribution in the F^2 generation is not in multiples of four as when one allelomorphic pair is in question, but in multiples of sixteen.

Every possible combination occurred in the second generation: nine TALL YELLOW; three TALL green; three dwarf YELLOW, and one dwarf green. Though the original parents were one of them TALL YELLOW and one of them dwarf green, in F^2, six out of sixteen offspring had combinations of traits not represented in the original parents, i.e. three TALL green and three dwarf YELLOW.

This biological principle which underlies new combinations of traits is known as the *independence of segregation* of unit characteristics; and though many facts in human inheritance are still obscure, it is certain that this principle is operative in human inheritance of allelomorphic pairs. Long-headedness and blondness have been singled out as Nordic characteristics, and broad-headedness and swarthiness as Alpine characteristics, but the fact that blondness splits off from long-headedness and broad-headedness from swarthiness is no longer a mystery. The map of physical forms in Europe, for instance, becomes only what one would expect after the mingling of all the

DIAGRAM II

Female Parent, F¹

Male Parent, F¹	TALL YELLOW	TALL green	dwarf YELLOW	dwarf green
TALL YELLOW	F² { TALL YELLOW / TALL YELLOW	F² { TALL green / TALL YELLOW	F² { dwarf YELLOW / TALL YELLOW	F² { dwarf green / TALL YELLOW
TALL green	F² { TALL YELLOW / TALL green	F² { TALL green / TALL green	F² { dwarf YELLOW / TALL green	F² { dwarf green / TALL green
dwarf YELLOW	F² { TALL YELLOW / dwarf YELLOW	F² { TALL green / dwarf YELLOW	F² { dwarf YELLOW / dwarf YELLOW	F² { dwarf green / dwarf YELLOW
dwarf green	F² { TALL YELLOW / dwarf green	F² { TALL green / dwarf green	F² { dwarf YELLOW / dwarf green	F² { dwarf green / dwarf green

diverse types that have gone into its ancestry. The more
unit characters in which parent types differ, the more
recombinations are possible in the second and later
generations. If we could isolate ten unit characters in
human beings, and the parents should differ in all ten,
there are 1022 combinations possible ($2^{10} = 1024$, minus
the parental pair, i.e. 1022). The human reproductive
cells are thus able to play countless variations upon the
original inheritance, and in all regions of the world they
have done so.

The question of pure races thus takes on a different
aspect in view of modern genetics. Physical anthropologists still often speak as if the question were one of
identifying the traits that belong to original human types,
i.e. of identifying a Nordic type in which narrow-headedness and blondness are bracketed. Then one student,
discussing a type which is narrow-headed and swarthy,
will deny its relationship to the Nordics on the basis of
its pigmentation, and another will "prove" the relationship on the basis of its cephalic index. The dispute waxes
bitter. But according to genetic principles both traits
are relevant; inheritance by its very nature constantly
produces types which are not duplicates of any ancestral
form. The particular series of traits any one student
may identify as a basic "type" is a convenience for
arranging his data rather than genetically significant.

The laws of genetics are also important for a knowledge
of human races because they lay the basis for the only
scientific means of identifying pure race as over against
mixed race. Mendelian principles make necessary an
entirely different method in the study of racial crossing.
As we have seen, when the father and mother are of
different physical types, the distribution of traits in the
offspring makes these offspring unlike each other, whereas
if the two parents are of the same type their offspring will

be alike. No human group has been observed where this latter condition occurs, i.e. where the brothers and sisters in a family present no significant differences one from the other. Hence all the human material we have indicates that, even in segregated communities, there is some multiple ancestry and some of the children incline toward one ancestral strain and some toward another. Racial purity, in the sense that all individuals have all the same traits, is not recorded, though it is possible that it existed before contact with Whites among some small groups of sub-arctic Eskimos who had been isolated for centuries. Racial purity in any human group can only mean that each fraternity (brothers and sisters born of one father and mother) duplicates every other fraternity in inherited traits; that is, that though, according to genetic principles, there will be some recombinations of traits within each fraternity, inbreeding has continued down the generations till all these fraternities resemble each other because they share the same inheritance. Among the mountain Whites in isolated Tennessee valleys; among the Bastaards of South Africa, a community whose ancestors were early European male colonists and Hottentot women; in the Malay Archipelago island of Kisar, a community descended from Dutch fathers and Malay mothers, all the fraternities in each group are genetically similar. The brothers and sisters in South Africa and in Kisar differ more within one fraternity than the mountain Whites, since their component strains are more diverse, but they have, by inbreeding, attained a high degree of racial homogeneity. If a physical anthropologist takes the measurements of one fraternity in these communities, he has closely approximated the measurements of all the fraternities, and one fraternity can stand as a very fair sample of all of them.

In any investigation of race this index is the one which reveals to us the degree to which a homogeneous race has been attained. It is not attained in urban centres of Europe, where many family lines having no correspondence one with the other are universally found, and where measurements of one fraternity cannot possibly stand as representative of other fraternities. But a homogeneous race, measured in this way, is the only "pure race" which has meaning within the human species. It is ironic that it is those very European nations in which anthropometric investigation shows no pure race which base their claims to superiority on allegations of their "pure" blood.

Genetics, in recent years, has made another essential contribution to the understanding of heredity. It has shown that new traits arise by mutation. Sometimes a fruit-fly or a calf is born with characteristics that are not due to its pooled heredity and it passes on this new characteristic to its offspring and their descendants. Herefords have been for a long time the most popular ranch cattle in the United States and Canada. When in 1889 a hornless calf was born on a Kansas farm, stock breeders recognized the advantage of ranch cattle without horns. From this Kansas calf have been bred all the present "polled" Herefords. The fact of mutations is today undeniable, and it is known that the likelihood of such occurrences is greatly increased by certain environmental conditions. For instance, it is increased under the influence of radiation at high altitudes, and, in the laboratory, by X-rays.

The older evolutionists assumed a quite different theory of the way in which new traits developed. Darwin believed in the inheritance of acquired characteristics. Giraffes grew longer and longer necks as they were forced to reach for higher and higher leaves, and each new generation, by hereditary transmission of this acquired trait, became longer-necked. Or fish in caves lost their eyesight through disuse and transmitted blindness to their descendants. In the human race, therefore, acquirements of parents were believed to be transmitted to their children.

Modern genetics has performed experiment after experiment, all of which show that Dàrwin and his contemporaries were mistaken. Inheritance of acquired characteristics does not occur. New traits are due to mutations, which occur even in the most closely bred lines. These mutations are haphazard and few of them could give to their possessor any possible advantage. The characteristic features of different races arose thus through mutation—blue eyes, for instance—and became characteristic of large populations by inbreeding in those "areas of characterization" where groups of the human race settled down in the early history of mankind. But the idea that the *achievements* of forefathers are passed on to their descendants by heredity is completely discredited. Heredity takes no notice of the glories of civilization, whether they are in science or in technology or in art; these can be perpetuated in any group, not by nature, but by nurture.

WHAT THEY SAY

The Biologists.

With full responsibility for my words as a professional biologist, I do not hesitate to say that all existing and genuine knowledge about the way in which the physical characteristics of human communities are related to their cultural capabilities can be written on the back of a postage stamp.

Lancelot Hogben, " Preface on Prejudices " in Cedric Dover, *Half-Caste*. London, Secker & Warburg, 1937, p. 9.

In regard to really important characteristics, the natural differences between the races pale into insignificance beside the natural differences between individuals —so much so that an impartial science of genetic improvement could not afford to take the former into account at all in its procedure.

H. J. Muller, *Out of the Night : a Biologist's View of the Future.* London, Gollancz, 1936.

When it is remembered that we are still uncertain whether hereditary differences have any part at all in causing the class differences in intelligence, while it cannot be denied that the environment has some hand in this, the priority of environmental over genetical methods of raising the general level of intelligence becomes obvious.

C. H. Waddington, *An Introduction to Modern Genetics.* London, Allen & Unwin, 1939, p. 358.

SIX

Who is Superior?

THE SCIENTIFIC STUDY of race tells us many important facts which have nothing to do with the question of the superiority or inferiority of given races. It tells us un- recorded and forgotten facts of early history and of the movement of peoples; it tells us what combinations of traits occur upon the mixture of two racial types; it distinguishes between a group of people who constitute a nation and a group of people who constitute a biological type (race). This scientific study of race has been an integral part of anthropology from its earliest beginnings because it provided a record, written in the bones and other bodily characteristics of men, of the history of man- kind; and in this study anthropologists have found over- whelmingly that race did not correlate with superiority or inferiority. From the great pioneer anthropologist Theodor Waitz, who examined the question in 1859, to the most recent studies of Franz Boas, they have reiterated that on this point the study of race gives only negative evidence.

Of all human questions, however, that of superiority and inferiority lies closest to the heart of man. He has always, like the simplest savages, called his own im- mediate concerns not simply dearest to him, but the most important in the universe; in a word, "superior." Whatever information comes to hand, he scans it for proofs of his belief. It was inevitable, therefore, that new facts about race should have been studied over and over again from this point of view. In this there was nothing that was peculiar to race; religions have been

similarly classified and absolute judgments pronounced;
so have class differences and sex differences, and differences between one grand duchy and a neighbouring one,
and between one nation and another; even when they
both have the same racial composition. With the growth
of knowledge about race after the middle of the nineteenth century, students attempted to find a scientific
basis on which to judge the innate superiority or inferiority of one racial group to another. Work was carried
on in three fields: physiological, psychological, and
historical.

Physiological.

The early evolutionists believed that man's physical
evolution had proceeded in a straight line from his pre-
human progenitors up to the White race. They considered the evolutionary process a ladder, each rung of
which had marked some advance upon the ape. Thus
the apes have broad, flat noses, as have also the Bushmen,
Negroes, and Australians; Europeans have narrow,
prominent noses. More prominent configuration of the
nose and lessened limb length were therefore end results
of evolution and were characteristic of the White race.

Investigations on the anatomical form of apes and
human beings have shown, during the last fifty years,
that the evolutionists' belief in a unilinear development
of human anatomy was mistaken. Both in anthropoids
and in human races special developments have occurred
locally which cannot be arranged in a unilinear series.
The most obvious differences between apes and men is
that between the hairy coat of the anthropoids and the
human skin. Of all human races the Mongoloids are the
freest of body hair; the Whites, along with the Australian
aborigines and some local tribes belonging to other races,

are the hairiest. The anthropoids have thin lips, and the most contrastingly "human" development is the full lips of the Negro; Whites have much more "primitive" lips. Neither by the test of hairiness nor by the test of lips would the Whites belong to that branch of the human race anatomically farthest removed from the ancestral type. No race has a monopoly of evolutionary end products, and no arguments for superiority can be based on single traits selected just because they favour the White race.

The most important contention of the early evolutionists was that superiority was manifest in the increasing size of the brain cavity. Apes have receding foreheads and small brains; men have prominent foreheads and large brains. Therefore the average brain size in any race would indicate its place on the evolutionary ladder. The average weight of the brain in proportion to total bodily weight is smaller among Negroes than among Mongoloids, and somewhat smaller among Mongoloids than among Whites. These differences are average differences, but the overlapping is so great that almost any individual human brain might belong to any of these three great races. Nor is the absolute difference great; human brain sizes, except for the pygmies, fall within a very small range as compared to the gap between man and the anthropoid apes. Boule [1] gives the maximum size for the latter as 621 cubic centimetres; whereas for Negroes he gives 1477 c.c. and for Parisians 1550 c.c. Pearson's series of European males, on the other hand, averages 1490 c.c.—almost the average Boule gives for Negroes—whereas Pearson finds that Negro males average 1350 c.c. [2] Figures for the human species there-

---

[1] Boule, Marcellin, *Fossil Man: Elements of Human Palæoethnology.* Translated from the French by Jessie E. and James Ritchie. Edinburgh, 1923. p. 229.

[2] Pearson in *Biometrika*, Vol. 8, 1912, pp. 292-337.

D

fore cluster together and are far removed from those for
the ancestral types. The only human brain sizes that are
to any marked degree intermediate are those of pygmy
races and tribes of very slight body build, and such brain
sizes are just one measurement among many which are
smaller because a smaller individual is being measured.
We are not justified in leaping without more proof to the
conclusion that this slighter build places them at a congenital *mental* disadvantage.

In all races where there is comparable body build,
brain sizes in one racial group overlap those of the others
except for the most extreme cases, and individuals whose
race is not known cannot be assigned to one race or
another on the basis of this measurement. The difference
between individuals in brain size is very great; the
difference between racial averages very small. Except
for the pygmy and semi-pygmy groups, the quarter of
the world's population having the largest brains would
include individuals from all races. It would be more
realistic, if we were really convinced of the importance
of this criterion, to favour all large-brained individuals
of whatever race.

But even this claim to *individual* superiority based on
brain size is doubtful. Very eminent Europeans have
had brains that were unusually small. The real point is
how the brain functions. So far as functioning has an
organic basis, it seems to depend not on gross size but on
the extent of the brain's surface area, which increases as
the brain has more convolutions. Almost nothing is
known of individual differences in the microscopic structure of the brain, and nothing at all is known of racial
differences.

Organic differences in the brain can never by themselves answer the question of superiority and inferiority.
In the absence of significant differences which set the

races of comparable body build apart from one another *as races*, the real problem in this matter, as in the study of any other human organ, is the relation between structure and function. Even in our own personal lives each of us knows the difference in functioning that may go along with one fixed identical organ. So long as no disease invades our lungs or our hearts, we each of us have the same lungs, the same heart, from the end of adolescence to senility. But the functioning of these organs varies greatly. When we climb mountains, our hearts pound and our breath comes short; when we compose ourselves for sleep, our heart-beats are slight and our breath long and regular. When we spend a summer at a high altitude or when we winter in the tropics, temporary changes take place. The heart structure or the lung structure has not changed; these organs merely have a considerable margin of safety so that they live within their means whether they function in one way or another. This circumstance, which we all have good reason to know in our own lives, is basic also when we compare groups of people. There too we find evidences of this same margin of safety. Races with low basal metabolism function in many regions alongside races with high basal metabolism, and this physiological difference does not prevent their adjustment. The eyesight of different peoples may test the same, yet some primitive peoples seem to White explorers to see as if they were using binoculars or microscopes; they have trained their eyes to serve in certain situations with such attention to minutiae that the result seems miraculous. On the other hand, primitive people find our ability to discriminate letters on a page equally miraculous; the difference is not in the organ but in the experiences in which the organ has habitually functioned.

The brain is not a case apart. People with brains of

similar structure may use them very differently, and this is also due to the various experiences in which their minds have habitually functioned. We should be guilty of the ultimate crudity if we confused hereditary structure with learned functioning. There are, of course, organic limits just as there are bad hearts and astigmatic eyes, but individuals with organically inferior brains are born in all races; no race as a whole is condemned to feeble-mindedness.

In all this discussion of brain size I have excepted the pygmy and semi-pygmy races. Whether these races could function in modern civilization is a purely academic question. It is not a live issue, for they are slated for destruction on social grounds. They have been pushed back into unwanted mountain fastnesses and deserts from regions which have been their hereditary homes. No one, I think, can look at the famous group of the little Bushman family by Malvina Hoffman without wanting to set the clock back and let them live out their lives in peace no matter what their brain size is. They were sufficiently gifted, at all events, to cover the rocks of their desert country with spirited paintings of animal hunts that excite the admiration of European painters today. Their old tribal ways of life were kindly and inoffensive. But to the early White farmer and cattleman their cardinal sin was that they refused to submit; to the last they resisted the encroachments of the stranger. Therefore they were killed on sight, as one contemporary put it, "by the powerful hand of the Ruler of heaven and earth," and it was only the occasional White outsider in those days who wrote that he was revolted by the wanton killing of these helpless men and women, and shocked at the administrator, otherwise so sensible a gentleman, who regarded it as a routine part of his daily work and ordained by Heaven. It was only an occasional traveller who marvelled at "the beautiful symmetrical form of our Bushman guide, who walked and sometimes ran before us with a gait the most free and easy I have ever beheld. His well-proportioned, although small and delicate figure, his upright and manly port, his firm, bold steps, and the consciousness of liberty which beamed in his countenance afforded us indescribable pleasure." [1]   The Bushmen might not have been able to adjust themselves to machine civilization, but in spite of their cranial capacity they were not a reproach to the human race.

Psychological.

Psychological tests of racial superiority are an attempt to apply less crude, more relevant standards than the mere gross size of the brain. They test some of the end results of the brain's functioning, and it is this question of what the brain can do which is crucial. There have been, therefore, a long series of psychological investigations during the last twenty-five years which have rated intelligence quotients of different racial and national groups as shown in their achievements in various kinds of individual and group tests.

Most intelligence testing has been done in America. During the first World War tests were given to the American Expeditionary Forces, and the enormous number of individuals from all sections of the country made this test population an ideal sampling compared to all earlier attempts. The scores on these tests were arranged by crude racial and national groupings— Negroes, Jews, persons of British or of Italian ancestry— and an average "mental age" for each group was derived. The differences were great. Whereas the average mental age of the White race in the army was 13·1 years, that

---

[1] Burchell, quoted in W. J. Sollas, *Ancient Hunters*. London, 1911, p. 272.

of the Negroes was 10·4, and the overlap was only 12 per cent.[1] Among the various immigrant White nationalities the Poles were at the bottom of the list; the Italians were on about the same level as the Poles.

The results of these army scores posed a problem on which the intelligence testers have been working ever since. The first reaction to the results was that here at last was an answer to the question of whether intelligence was transmitted by inheritance. Terman, one of the early investigators, had described the Binet test as giving a measure of innate intelligence scarcely influenced by education and experience. Brigham, who interpreted the army tests on immigrants from different parts of Europe, concluded that, since the scores of individuals of Northern European ancestry were higher than those of Southern European ancestry, Nordics had more innate intelligence than Alpines and Mediterraneans. The low scores of Negroes were held to measure directly their congenital inferiority to the Whites.

Work during the last decade, however, has led racial psychologists to doubt this conclusion. The intelligence tests were of several different kinds. Some were highly verbal, including vocabulary as one item of the test. It was obvious that those who spoke English at home and used it easily scored higher than those who spontaneously expressed themselves in another language. Many of the words in the vocabulary and some of those in the directions given the person taking the test were not used commonly in the vernacular and could be known to children from many homes only from book knowledge. Negroes and recent immigrants or children of foreign-born parentage were at a disadvantage. Such a language handicap was

---

[1] Yerkes, R. M., " Psychological Examining in the United States Army," *Memoir of the National Academy of Sciences*. Washington, Vol. 15, vi, 1921, p. 790.

obviously not congenital, and this fact had to be taken into account before the value of the tests as measures of innate ability could be considered.

The testers also stressed another difficulty, not only in the army tests but in all subsequent testing. The results are comparable for two groups only when both are interested in doing as well as they can. The differences in this particular are only too apparent to the tester, and they influence the results. Garth even suggests, instancing the high scores of the Japanese and Chinese tested in America—intelligence quotients of 99 as against the Whites' 100—that perhaps the reason the Negroes, Mexicans, and Indians did so poorly in comparison was that they could not "take the white man's seriousness seriously." [1] The Stanford-Binet test is indeed far from resembling anything which is to them traditionally important.

There are even more specific differences among different groups in this matter of doing as well as they can. Good manners differ in different cultures in ways which influence the tests. Among many peoples, and especially among American Indian tribes, a person is trained never to answer a question or state a fact except when he is absolutely and unassailably sure of himself. Any minor uncertainty, which an American school child typically takes very lightly, will render him dumb. His great humiliation comes, not like our children's, from being slow or backward in answering, but from having ventured at all unless he was on completely firm ground. He will not retell the little test story at all unless he can cover each detail; he will not interpret the picture if there is a "Western Union" envelope in it which he never saw before. Klineberg [2] remarks on the difficulties

---

[1] Garth, Thomas Russell, *Race Psychology, a Study of Racial Mental Differences*. London, McGraw Hill, 1931, p. 183.
[2] Klineberg, Otto, *Race Differences*. London, Harper, 1935, p. 155.

caused by the Dakota Indians' good manners, which
taboo giving any answer in the presence of someone who
does not know the answer. Tests made among children
with such rules of politeness are not really comparable
with tests made in another culture where there is a taboo
against presuming to answer in the presence of someone
who *does* know the answer, and with tests made in our
culture, where most children will try to give an answer
under any circumstances. In societies where great defer-
ence is accorded to chiefs or high castes any group test
situation is hopelessly distorted. In all these cases the
rules of etiquette influence the scores.

There are endless difficulties of all kinds. In the test
of matching colours the Balinese children spent all their
time putting harmonious colours together "for a pretty
belt." The Balinese are very sophisticated about colour
and they could not accept the idea of wasting time
putting the *same* colours together when they might be
showing their taste in colour arrangement. The commonest difficulty in the colour tests in other societies is
that the categories of colours differ so widely. The spec-
trum is a colour continuum with no sharp breaks anywhere; the English language draws a line at one point
and we see "yellow" on one side of that line and "green"
on the other. Another language decrees a dividing line
at another point, somewhere, let us say, between light
green and dark green, and it calls the light green *and
certain yellows* both "young leaves colour," and the dark
greens *and certain blues* both "shaded water colour."
Their grouping of colours is as reasonable as ours, but
their test performances cannot be rated on the same scale
as ours. Certain other cultural peculiarities are not so
easy to correct as the colour categories. In word tests,
like those of "opposites," the Samoans attained very
high scores. They are accustomed in their culture to

verbal play, to puns, to epigrams. In other test situations, their performances often failed miserably according to our standards, just as the Balinese failed in matching colours.

Even granting the doubts that were raised about the test themselves and the growing belief among testers that the results gave an indication of scholastic achievement rather than of innate intelligence, the chief doubt which gained ground was whether the results indicated *racial* differences or were only so presented that they seemed to do so. The scores whether for Whites or Negroes were obviously not the same from different parts of the country. It was worth investigating whether the differences were sectional. The testers therefore tabulated the Whites of Southern states as against the Negroes of Northern states and the results were startling—arranged by median scores Southern Whites fell below Northern Negroes.

WHITES [1]

Mississippi	41·25
Kentucky	41·50
Arkansas	41·55

NEGROES

New York	45·02
Illinois	47·35
Ohio	49·50

Such a breakdown of the results showed a fundamental fallacy in the original interpretation. The Negroes of the United States are massed in the South; their I.Q. (intelligence quotient) was significant not only in so far as they were *Negroes* but as *Southerners*. Obviously even

[1] *Op. cit.,* p. 182.

the dominant White race did badly in the tests if they had been reared in certain Southern states, where per capita expenditures for education are low and the low standard of living is revealed in every survey and to every casual visitor. The testers felt that there was reasonable doubt concerning conclusions of inherent racial differences, and they gave further tests. They tested Negro and White boys in Nashville, then in Chicago, and then in New York City. The Negro scores were farthest below the White in Nashville, somewhat below in Chicago, and equalled the White score in New York City. They tried Los Angeles, where Negroes are few in number and are educated in the same classrooms with Whites; their average I.Q. was 104·7 (as over against an average I.Q. for the Southern Negro of about 75),[1] and this was "slightly above that of the White children with whom they were compared." The results of the tests varied with educational opportunity.

Some testers still believed that these results cast no fundamental doubt on the original interpretation because only superior Negroes had gone North or West. This explanation is called "selective migration." The testers therefore examined school records in Southern cities to find evidence that the brightest boys went North. The average of all emigrants to the North was almost exactly the average for the whole Negro school population in those cities.[2] Then they tested Negro school children in New York schools; if the high average they attained was due to the fact that only the cream of the Southern Negro population came North, the length of time they had been in New York would have no influence on their scores. But the lowest I.Q.'s were those of the newest arrivals, and length of residence strongly affected the

---

[1] Garth, *op. cit.*, p. 219.
[2] Klineberg, *ibid.*, pp. 185-186.

scores. There was still a further question to be answered: could it be that the newer arrivals from the South were inferior to the earlier? Tests were given and the results showed that it was the other way round: in the groups sampled the later migrants made the better scores. All that was left, therefore, was the correlation between test scores and social and educational advantages. The environmental advantages of the Negro in the United States never equalled those of the Whites of the same economic level, but wherever they became more similar the "inferiority" of the Negro tended to disappear.

Intelligence testers therefore have swung to an interpretation of their data radically different from that of the 1920's. As Thorndike put it as far back as 1914: "The facts [i.e. data on I.Q.'s of different races and nationalities] are measurements of differences between groups which are distinct to an unknown degree in traits which are influenced by training to an unknown degree." [1] Garth, whose life was largely given to racial testing and whose book is a standard reference on the subject, says that, though his work began with "a silent conviction that he would find clear-cut racial differences in mental processes," he came, from a consideration of all psychological tests, to the conclusion that "it is useless to speak of the worthlessness of so-called 'inferior peoples' when their worth has never been established by a fair test." [2] Klineberg, whose *Racial Differences* contains a clear summary of mental testing, concludes: "Intelligence tests may therefore not be used as measures of group differences in native ability, though they may be used profitably as measures of accomplishment. When comparisons are made within the same race or group, it can

---

[1] Thorndike, E. L., *Educational Psychology*, Vol. III. New York, 1921, p. 207.
[2] Garth, *op. cit.*, pp. vii and 101.

be demonstrated that there are very marked differences
depending upon variations in background. These differences may be satisfactorily explained, therefore, without
recourse to the hypothesis of innate racial differences in
mental ability." [1] Even Brigham, whose interpretation
of the army tests in 1921 was that they showed racial
superiority of the Nordic over the Alpine and Mediterranean, has reversed his conclusion. In 1930 he
wrote: "Comparative studies of various national and
racial groups may not be made with existing tests. . . .
In particular, one of the most pretentious of these comparative racial studies—the writer's own—was without
foundation." [2]

The intelligence testers at the present time, therefore,
regard their data as indicating achievement and primarily
scholastic achievement. For this both innate aptitude
and specific training are necessary; in other words, both
heredity and environment play their parts. The problem
is whether the hereditary factor is a *racial constant*. The
results of racial tests are believed today to show that
hereditary aptitude is not distributed by races and that
when environmental conditions for different groups
become similar, average achievement also becomes
similar. Individual differences will still remain in all
races, but the results indicate that any programme which
proposes to increase human achievement will attain its
ends by providing adequate and continued opportunity
for any individual without regard to race or colour. As
the biologist H. J. Muller puts it: "In . . . really important characteristics the natural differences between
the races pale into insignificance beside the natural
differences between individuals—so much so that an

[1] Klineberg, *op. cit.*, p. 189.
[2] Brigham, C. C., "Intelligence Tests of Immigrant Groups," *Psychological Review*, Vol. XXXVII. Princeton, 1930, p. 165.

impartial science of genetic improvement could not afford to take the former into account at all in its procedure." [1]

The whole procedure in the racial psychological tests has been ill-adapted to its original goal, even if the tests themselves had been unassailable. The goal was to discover the relative capacity of races. The animal breeder has the same sort of problem: he wants to find good breeds which are more worth encouraging than others. He does not decide on good performance by averaging all bulls of one breed regardless of the conditions under which they have lived. He knows that if his best specimen is sent to an unfamiliar range and given no care it will do nothing but sulk. This does not make him lose faith in the breed. He knows that his recommendations are not invalidated even though bad herding conditions will ruin his animals. He would not understand the method of the old psychological tester who presented averages of racial groups no matter under what conditions they lived. One good performance of his breed would outweigh for him whole series where it had done badly; his one fine bull would make him alert to duplicate the success, since obviously the breed was capable under certain conditions of such performance.

So, too, in the psychological tests, if we are as much in earnest about human capabilities as the farmer is about the cattle he breeds, we will give more weight to isolated achievements than to averages. Individual instances are not only more interesting than averages; they are in this case more pertinent. In the Pintner Non-Language Test, a full-blooded Indian girl of twelve from the United States Indian School at Santa Fé rated an I.Q. of 145, which is 45 points above the White average and more than 70 points above the Indian average. In the National

[1] Muller, H. J., *Out of the Night : a Biologist's View of the Future.* London, Gollancz, 1936, p. 120.

Intelligence Test, a Mexican boy in the public schools of
San Antonio obtained the same I.Q. of 145, outdistancing
the White average by just as much as the Indian girl and
outdistancing the average Mexican in the United States
by 67 points.[1] If these stocks can produce individuals
who do as well as this in meeting the requirements of
the test even under the conditions the Indian and the
Mexican have to meet in America, the *stocks* are not at
fault. In all stocks individuals differ in ability, and
civilization will always be the poorer if we close the gates
of opportunity to those of superior ability whatever their
blood may be.

Historical.

Claims of racial superiority have also been based on
history. It has been said that the rise and fall of civilization are due to race, that in accounting for progress or
deterioration one has only to examine the racial composition of the people. Eminent historians have many times
protested against this misrepresentation of history. We
need only to remember how many factors operated to
bring about the change, for instance, from the twelfth
to the thirteenth century or from the eighteenth to the
nineteenth; change in the racial composition of any
country, on the contrary, was negligible. Nevertheless
German racist policy today is principally based on this
pseudo-historical claim; Germany's enforcement of
racial hygiene and its drastic penalties against mixing
blood of Aryans and non-Aryans are put forward as
measures dictated by history. Politicians and educators
in the Third Reich reiterate constantly that pure race is
the secret of great civilizations. The answer to this is
that no people of high civilization have been racially

[1] Garth, *op. cit.*, p. 217.

pure; it is just as true to say that their rise was due to intermixture. The mingling of ethnic types began before the dawn of history and has always accompanied civilization both in periods of great achievement and in periods of retrogression. A constant factor cannot be the cause either of one or of the other.

A variant of this racist argument from history is that the Caucasian race has been responsible for all progress wherever it has appeared, whether in India, China, Mesopotamia, or Egypt, and that this is not due to exchange of knowledge and the stimulus of mutual intercourse, but to the inevitable operation of congenital superiority in the Caucasian. More commonly the claim is made for the Nordic subdivision of the White race. Thus Greece and Rome, though they were predominantly non-Nordic, owed their greatness to individuals who, it is maintained, were Nordic.

We have already examined this special pleading. It is not history, and historians have over and over again disavowed it. Modern civilization has been built upon the inventions of a great array of different ethnic groups, and many of the greatest of these inventions were made when the people of Europe were still backward barbarians and the Nordics were still unheard of in the great centres of population. The whole argument ignores historic processes and substitutes for them an unashamed racial megalomania.

This argument is, besides, a contradiction of the "pure" races argument, though the racists commonly put them forward together. If advances in civilization are due to the presence of a handful of Caucasians or Nordics who have leavened the whole loaf, this means inevitably a mixed race, which in this case is adduced by racists as the cause not of decline, but of rise, of civilizations. This difficulty they meet by a travesty of fact. It is said

that the reason this leavening had such good effects is
that a race manifests in all its history the same innate
mental and emotional characteristics. Thus the Teutons
(read *Nordics*) have always been loyal to their chosen
leaders, they have always been adventurous, they have
always been conquerors. Whatever the period of past
history, whatever the future may bring, these qualities
are innate in the breed *and in no other*.

History has itself answered this argument on a grand
scale. From two points of view history refutes this argument. In the first place, the racist who claims for the
whole White race innate powers to progress in civilization does not attempt to prove conspicuous achievement
for the whole White race. He is always speaking of the
sample of the White race or the Nordic race with which
he identifies himself. The peasants of Central and
Southern Europe are as much a part of the White race
as the aristocracy or the urban population, but their
ways of procuring a livelihood, their narrow horizons in
intellectual and social matters, are to the objective
student less "civilized" than those of many Negro and
Mongoloid "primitives." The Scotch-English of purest
White race who settled in the Tennessee and Kentucky
highlands did not by the fact of their race become leaders
of civilization; their endless and bloody family feuds,
their illiterateness, their preservation of old ballads make
them picturesque and appealing to those who know them,
but their racial descent did not cause them to advance
civilization.

When the claim is made for the Nordic sub-race, the
position is equally untenable. A German racist in describing Nordics speaks not of Nordics in Scandinavia,
England, France, and America, but of *German* Nordics;
a Frenchman speaks of *French* Nordics—or he discounts
the claims of Nordic supremacy and says the same things

about Gallo-Romans (read *Celts*, *Alpines*). The lesson of history is that under favourable conditions there have been adventurers and conquerors in every race and sub-race; any list of virtues that can be drawn up has had exponents in every race in some period of its history and in some social situations.

History refutes this argument of an inalienable racial soul in still another way. The racial composition of Europe changes slowly, far too slowly to account by itself for the rapid changes in social behaviour which history records. The England of Elizabeth and of Shakespeare changed in one man's lifetime to the England of Cromwell. The England of the Restoration, which is portrayed so vividly in Pepys' *Diary*, gave way again, in another lifetime, to the England of the eighteenth century. We can trace the causes in political and social conditions but not in any change of racial composition. It has been the same in Spain, in France, in Germany, and in Italy. Whatever lists of striking achievements or mental and emotional characteristics can be drawn up, no one set of these is automatically perpetuated over time by the "blood" of any people. They change rapidly with a social change from political and economic security to insecurity; they change, we often say, begging the question, with "the atmosphere of the times." But rapid changes in Europe cannot be traced to changes in racial composition.

This is just as true of the non-European world. Racially Japan has been for centuries much more stable than Europe. After centuries of Oriental civilization she has in the last decades adopted Occidental standards with fervour and success. This right-about-face is in no way due to a change in the racial composition of Japan, though it can be accounted for in detail, as Sydney L. Gulick showed as early as 1903 in his *Evolution of the*

Japanese, by taking account of social changes. As he says, if the racists believe that both these periods in Japanese history are due to an unalterable psychic constitution inherent in the race, it is incumbent on them to state what these inalienable characteristics are that overspan these periods. The racists were too precipitate. Le Bon said, in proving the permanent biological character of the Japanese: "A Japanese may easily take a university degree or become a lawyer; the sort of varnish he thus acquires is, however, quite superficial and has no influence on his mental constitution. What no education can give him, because they are created by heredity alone, are the forms of thought, the logic, and above all the character of Western Man." [1] At the present day the usual complaint is that Japan has too successfully taken over the character of the Western Powers. She has not, in Le Bon's phrase, "shown a mental constitution as unvarying as her anatomical characteristics." To get around this difficulty, Japan's "mental constitution" itself was a decade or so ago often described as fickle and given to a series of fads. This description is not common now that the Japanese are so well launched on their modern career; it is still more strikingly inapplicable to the fifteen hundred years of the old military social order that ended in the middle of the last century. In those centuries the permanence and fixity of Japanese life were greatly in excess of anything of which we have record in Europe. What was called innate fickleness at the turn of this century was evidently a temporary manifestation which accompanied rapid social readjustment. Another favourite description of the innate behaviour of the Japanese was that it was ceremonious and at the opposite pole from the purposefully ordered conduct of Occidentals. Sir Edwin Arnold said the Japanese of his day

[1] Le Bon, Gustave, *The Psychology of Peoples*. London, 1898, p. 37.

had "the nature rather of birds and butterflies than of ordinary human beings"—by which of course he meant Europeans. Now we talk about the Japanese as subordinating themselves to their purposes more abjectly than the superior Europeans. At least the purposes of modern Japan are those the Western World also pursues, and we are therefore able to recognize them.

Historically the right-about-face of Japanese culture from its slow-moving ceremonious ways of life, its high appreciation of aesthetic values, its feudal organization and military caste system—from these to its modern bustle, its dedication to commerce and imperialistic wars—was dramatically explicit and man-made. Japan recognized that the Western foreigners could not always be kept at arm's length by continued policies of exclusion, and she decided on a different course. She determined to learn from them all they had to teach and thus to put herself in a position of equality. Therefore, in 1868 the Emperor in the first year of this new "enlightened" policy—as it is called in Japan—stated in his edict: "The old uncivilized way shall be replaced. . . . The best knowledge shall be sought throughout the world, so as to promote the Imperial welfare." This social change has been carried out with enthusiasm, and can be seen reflected in the manifold developments in Japan up to the present time. These developments have proceeded at an extremely rapid pace in spite of the "Oriental mentality" which had formerly characterized Japan. Yet Japan's race is still Mongoloid as it has always been. She belies Le Bon's pronouncement: "Cross-breeding is the only infallible means at our disposal of transforming in a fundamental manner the character of a people, heredity being the only force powerful enough to contend with heredity." [1]

[1] *Ibid.*, p. 83.

Swift and radical changes in mental and emotional behaviour without an accompanying change of race occur constantly in native cultures when they come into conflict with White civilization. The American Indian of the Great Plains was a proud and undaunted warrior. His resourcefulness and courage, his eloquence, his generosity won the admiration of explorers and traders in the early days. With the expansion of White settlement, the buffalo, his mainstay of life, was slaughtered, and he could no longer procure food. His land was taken from him. The White men, unless at the moment they were using him as an ally in war, found it to their advantage to make his feats of bravery offences punishable by bloody reprisals. His culture collapsed about him like a house of cards. Within a generation his independence and vigorous assertiveness were lost. His "racial soul" availed him nothing. Under the changed conditions he became the lacklustre drunkard and beggar the full-bloods are all too often today on our reservations. There were, of course, honourable exceptions, but these exceptions were also cases of equally radical changes in psychic constitution. The old behaviour pattern did not live on either in the morally and psychically broken Indians nor in those who were able under even the most difficult circumstances to adjust themselves to modern conditions.

The most drastic change of this sort is, however, that which took place in a generation or two among the Negroes brought to America as slaves. Most of them had been transported from Nigerian kingdoms with prized cultural achievements. Their elaborate and ceremonious political organization, the pomp of their courts, the activity of their far-flung economic life with its great market centres and tribute collected over great areas, their legal systems with formal trial of the accused, with witnesses and with prosecutors—all these excite the admiration of any student. Belatedly we admire today the incisive folk-tales of Nigeria, their rhythmic dances, their wood-carving that has excited the respect of modern European artists. But these are today collected in Africa. In America all this achievement was stripped from imported slaves as if they had never had part in it. Their patterns of political, economic, and artistic behaviour were forgotten—even the languages they had spoken in Africa. Like the poor Whites of the South, they gathered together instead for fervent Christian revivalist camp meetings; they sang the hymns the poor Whites sang, and if they sang them better and invented countless variations of great poignancy, nevertheless the old forms which they had achieved in Africa were forgotten. Conditions of slavery in America were so drastic that this loss is not to be wondered at. The slaves on any one plantation had come from tribes speaking mutually unintelligible languages and with mutually unfamiliar arts of life; they had been herded together like cattle in slave ships and sold at the block in a strange and frightening world. They were worked hard on the plantations. It is no wonder that their owners remarked upon their lack of any cultural achievements; the mistake they made was to interpret the degradation of the slave-trade as if it were an innate and all-time characteristic of the African Negro. The Negro race has proud cultural achievements, but for very good reasons they were not spread before our eyes in America.

Radical and rapid changes in mental and emotional behaviour, whether we consider them to be in the direction of progress or of deterioration, give the lie to the racists' contention that these patterns are eternal and are biologically perpetuated. They are reversed with reversals in social conditions and demands.

One further contention of superiority is put forward by the racists. It is simple in the extreme. "The Whites are today the most 'civilized'; therefore their 'blood' is superior." This is a non-sequitur of the kind we examined a moment ago, for higher civilization is not a characteristic of *all* Whites but only of certain areas of White civilization. To understand the development of elaborate forms of civilization we have to turn to historical, not to biological, facts. History cannot be explained so simply. There is no law of the rate of cultural progress—let alone a biological law. The history of all civilizations, whether they are Caucasian or Malay or Mongol, shows periods of great vigour, and also periods of stability and even ossification. Since this is a general phenomenon, it is not necessary to invoke a special innate superiority of the White race to account for the present epoch of great Caucasian vigour. The particular direction White civilization has taken in the past centuries— successful control of the material world—has given it predominance in our times, but we do not know what the future will be. Our civilization has invented many things which White intelligence has not shown the ability to handle for our own obvious interests. Surely this, too, is a test of intelligence and one in which Western civilization has not distinguished itself. We may possibly go down in history as a prime example of a great civilization which for want of a little intelligence destroyed itself at great social cost. Claims of innate Caucasian intelligence are only self-congratulation at a moment in history when it is dangerous to be misled by flattering phrases. Nothing biological guarantees to any human group the perpetuation of its triumphs.

There is one final argument for racial superiority which is advanced after all those we have just reviewed are rejected. This argument is that the best Caucasians, however few, are better than any other men; and since they are the leaders and the inventors, the higher destiny of the Caucasian is assured. To support this position Professor Hankins adduces only evidence from brain size and weight and the earlier racial interpretations of the intelligence tests,[1] and for both of these we have already examined the evidence as it is assayed by scientists today. However, the "great man" theory still arises in racial discussion. As Professor Hankins puts it: "The frequency of superior individuals born within the group is of the greatest significance for the rôle of that group in cultural evolution." [2]

The "great man" theory of history had a spectacular development in the hands of Carlyle and is now generally held to be either inadequate or naïve. Sociologists do not say today as one did in 1921: "In the long run supremacy will pass in every community, nation, or race to the more intelligent, the more capable, the more ethical." It is a pious wish and true of some societies. But it depends upon what that society rewards with prestige. Great nations are directed at the present moment by individuals who have none of the qualifications mentioned by the optimistic sociologist of twenty years ago. Even if we grant the sense in which these leaders are indeed "superior individuals"—for at least they maintain themselves in power—we cannot therefore say that they have administered civilization to advantage. In our generation nations and communities have been ravaged by superior force of arms, and cultural progress has been compromised by these same "superior individuals." Race, moreover, has no specific bearing on whether or not a leader will arise who can take the helm

[1] Hankins, Frank H., *The Racial Basis of Civilization*. London, Knopf, 1927, pp. 308-319, 364-366.
[2] *Ibid.*, p. 305.

and prevent cultural catastrophe. No racial measurements will guarantee that Germany will have an intelligent leader and China an unintelligent one. The course of history is much too complex. We cannot trust our hopes for civilization to the "great man" theory in racial biology.

Why Cultures Differ.

Race, therefore, cannot account for all human differences. Nevertheless, the differences between a Frenchman and a German, a Chinese and a European, remain and are apparent to everyone. If race does not explain them, what does? Until we have some clear understanding of the processes which produce such different people, we may still in a pinch fall back on the racial explanation.

The human animal has, in comparison with all other animals, the widest range of potentialities. What he will become depends upon what potentialities his environment calls forth. His inherited traits are not specific, as a bird's are, for building a mud nest or a twig nest; they are extremely plastic. "Instinct" in man can be studied only in the protean forms it has taken as a result of the way a person was brought up as a child and the opportunities he has had as an adult to act in one way and not in another. His inherited tendencies are still present, but they do not operate as they do in birds or ants to lay down inexorably his whole way of life. It is on this fundamental fact that human achievements have all been built, for man's plasticity has proved to be even in the matter of self-defence a greater asset than strength to the lion or size to the elephant. It created the essential situation in which intelligence could be developed.

This plasticity, therefore, should be man's proudest boast. It follows that man reacts to his environment more completely and more quickly than any other creature. In an undeveloped country where he must meet conditions single-handed he is a pioneer, self-reliant and courageous. In an industrial city he performs one operation, continuously repeated, for eight hours a day (if he can find work, that is). In America his own father may have been the pioneer and he and his brothers, in spite of their inheritance, the machine operators. The machine operator's son may perhaps get an education and become an academic notable, spending his life in the library and the classroom and turning out books on philosophy or sociology. Inherited traits have passed directly from father to son down the generations, but the different traits that were developed in each individual of the family line were due to the environment in which he found himself.

The influence of environment on any one individual, however, is limited by his life-span. "Three-score years and ten" is a short time, and civilizations have sometimes had hundreds of years in which special influences were brought to bear consistently on generation after generation. Whether they have had centuries in which to foster particular ways of living, or only two generations, societies have always been overwhelmingly effective in moulding human material in different ways. Man is a highly gregarious animal and he always wants the approval of his fellows. First, of course, he has to get the means of keeping alive, but after that he will try to get approval in forms which his society recognizes. His society may recognize conquest, and he will engage in conquest; it may recognize wealth, and he will measure success by dollars and cents; it may recognize caste, and he will behave in all things according to the position to

which he was born. There are always, of course, recal-
citrant individuals who may perhaps persist in becoming
artists when society regards artists as feeble-minded, or
tyrants when society will not tolerate tyrants. These
recalcitrants are always most numerous in times of up-
heaval; eventually, the great majority in any continuing
civilization take the mould which is set by cultural
institutions.

Social anthropology is the study of such cultural
institutions. Every little tribe awards special approval
—some to this achievement, some to that—and the tribal
institutions allow men to pursue the favoured goal. If
this goal is deeds of daring, the individual character
fostered in that tribe is hardy and scornful of pain; if the
goal is to raise a good crop in one's garden, man is
industrious and patient of routine. There is incredible
variety in these goals, and most societies honour several
different kinds of achievement, usually compatible one
with another; whatever the goals are and the social
institutions which allow people to pursue them, human
behaviour is modified in conformity to them.

The social institutions of any one tribe are not inevitable expressions of racial genius, for other tribes of the
same race have radically different ones. The rugged
individualism of American Indian tribes of the western
plains on the one hand, and, in great contrast, the mild-
ness and sobriety of some Pueblo Indians on the other,
are both responses to the different ways of arranging
social life and the different opportunities for the individual provided by the two cultures. Both groups are
racially American Indians. The contrast between the
high civilization which Cortez found in Mexico and the
culture of tiny wandering groups of root-diggers and seed-
gatherers in the great basin between the Sierras of
California and Colorado was, again, not based on race.

American Indians were responsible for the one as well as for the other. In Mexico social behaviour responded to the more complex conditions which had grown up historically in that country.

The social environment in our own cultural background as well as in the primitive world has been favourable now to one kind of achievement, now to another. For a brief moment of time in the Age of Pericles, Athens accorded great liberty to the free-born Athenian; it honoured intellectual examination of all questions and the creation of art forms both in sculpture and in the drama. We have wondered ever since at the achievements a tiny city made in only two generations. The moment passed; social conditions changed. No "racial" superiority availed to carry the torch down the generations once civilization had moved on. In what we might almost call a fortunate accident men had shown what they might achieve under favourable conditions.

Conditions since the days of Athens have been favourable, now in one place and now in another, for certain achievements. The Renaissance in Italy was favourable for the development of art, and no one who has read the *Autobiography* of Benvenuto Cellini will wonder at the great efflorescence of art in those days. Cellini may have exaggerated the court paid to him as an artist by princes, but we know that the picture is essentially true to the times. Many kinds of intellectual activity, however, were definitely discouraged, as we know from the notebooks and life of Leonardo da Vinci. What opposition intellectual achievement of the wrong sort could arouse in high quarters, if it was pursued, has been made famous in the story of the trial of Galileo by the Inquisition.

In modern times there have also been now and again periods of great freedom and well-being, directed, however, not so much toward the intellectual life the Greeks rated so highly or the artistic creation the Florentines honoured, as toward the conquest of the material world and the acquisition of wealth. In these fields we have achieved the great and characteristic success of modern times, and the personality type which can best succeed in this endeavour has become increasingly prevalent, with various modifications, in nation after nation. The attainments that are honoured and the opportunities of reaching goals differ in the various nations and still more in different classes in each nation, and these differences we sum up in catch-phrases of "what the Irish are like" or "what the Italians are like," "what peasants are like" or "what bankers are like." All these characterizations are crude sketches of these groups as they are shaped by immediate conditions and have no valid pretensions as descriptions of innate characteristics which would persist under different conditions.

The racists have claimed superiority for this race or for that. But superiority has never been perpetuated in any community by mere germ plasm. Wherever we look in the past history of Western civilization, we find that favoured groups have achieved brief, brilliant success when they were assured economic sufficiency and freedom and opportunity in certain directions. When these favourable conditions no longer existed the torch soon fell from their hands. In the past the social conditions which have favoured achievement, now here, now there, have been limited to a certain class, like the free-born citizens of Athens, usually reckoned as one-seventh of the population, or the court and its satellites in England under Elizabeth. With growing literacy and extension of voting privileges and the spread of common ideas up and down the whole scale of the population in modern nations, this selective restriction of social opportunities no longer works so satisfactorily as it did in earlier times.

In America we have systematically destroyed the serf mentality which looked upon overlords as a world apart and regarded the poverty and dependence of underlings as part of the ways of God. Even in Europe there is a comparable situation in the more advanced states. They are faced with two alternatives: they must keep down the rank and file by the use of naked force, or they must see to it that the major goods of life are available to a much greater proportion of the population than in earlier European history. We are far from having made economic sufficiency general in America, and essential liberties—opportunity to work, freedom of opinion on moot points, and equality of civil liberties—are far from won. They are, however, not unattainable if we will bend our efforts to achieve them, and we have a much clearer idea than we had a decade ago of the measures that would have to be taken. If we are serious in our hopes for the human race, we will devote ourselves to providing those social conditions under which it can fulfil itself, and we shall not blindly trust the racists' flattery that the highest attainments will always be ours however we muddle through in our social life.

WHAT THEY SAY

Of all vulgar modes of escaping from the consideration of the effect of social and moral influences on the human mind, the most vulgar is that of attributing the diversities of conduct and character to inherent natural differences.

> John Stuart Mill, *Principles of Political Economy*. London, Longmans, Green & Co.

"Race" is the cheap explanation tyros offer for any collective trait that they are too stupid or too lazy to trace to its origin in the physical environment, the social environment, or historical conditions.

E. A. Ross, *Social Psychology*. London, Macmillan & Co., 1915, p. 3.

Heredity may explain a part of the pronounced mental similarities between parents and children; but this explanation cannot be transferred to explain on hereditary grounds the similarity of behaviour of entire nations in which the most varied lines occur. These assume their characteristic forms under the pressure of society.

Franz Boas, *Aryans and Non-Aryans*. New York, Information and Service Associates, 1934, p. 11.

[Cultural differences exist and have been emphasized in this volume] but they are only passing products of the milieu. Having come about as the result of external circumstances, they disappear in the same way.

Jean Finot, *Race Prejudice*. Translated by Florence Wade-Evans. London, Archibald Constable & Co., 1906, p. 317.

We have seen in detail that every characteristically Japanese moral trait is due to the nature of her past social order and is changing with that order. Racial moral traits, therefore, are not due to inherent nature, to essential character, to brain structure, nor are they transmitted from father to son by the mere fact of physical generation. On the contrary, the distinguishing ethical characteristics of races . . . are determined by the dominant social order, and vary with it.

Sydney L. Gulick, *The Evolution of the Japanese*. London, F. H. Revell, 1903, p. 285.

Men indeed differ in learning but are equal in the

capacity for learning; there is no race which under the guidance of reason cannot attain to virtue.

Cicero, first century B.C.

If we were to select the most intelligent, imaginative, energetic, and emotionally stable third of mankind, all races would be represented.

Franz Boas, *Anthropology and Modern Life.* London, Allen & Unwin, 1929, p. 75.

PART II: RACISM

SEVEN

A Natural History of Racism

RACE IS A SUBJECT which can be investigated by genealogical charts, by anthropomorphic measurements, by studies of the same zoological group under different conditions, and by reviews of world history. It can be investigated from the point of view of anthropometrists, genealogical experts, geneticists, and historians. In other words, it is a scientific field of inquiry and its special problem is that of genetic relationship of human groups. It ranks as an important field in any study of human civilizations and concerns itself with important facts about the history of the world. It tells us, for instance, from the skulls and bones of living races, about migrations of prehistoric peoples over two continents. It is the evidence upon which we base our knowledge of many facts of history. It tells us, as we have seen, that the Manchu rulers of China were by blood a rude Palaeo-asiatic tribe—a racial family with members who remained primitive herdsmen—and that the strain of the Hamites, so prominent in dynastic Egypt, is also represented by modern primitive tribes like the Galla and Somali.

Race is not "the modern superstition," as some amateur egalitarians have said. It is a fact. The study of it has already told culture-historians much, and further investigations, for which as yet science has not the necessary basic knowledge or tests, may even show that some ethnic groups have identifiable emotional or intellectual peculiarities which are biological and not merely learned behaviour. For example, certain ethnic groups show different *averages* in measurements of some hereditary glandular condition or metabolic peculiarity although each group contains many individuals who fall within a range common to all groups. History, however, has already shown, in instance after instance, that any such specializations, if they occur, leave such groups within a "margin of safety" sufficient so that any race, when opportunity has offered, has adjusted itself to the most contrasting cultures and participated in them.

Race, then, is not the modern superstition. But racism is. Racism is the dogma that one ethnic group is condemned by nature to congenital inferiority and another group is destined to congenital superiority. It is the dogma that the hope of civilization depends upon eliminating some races and keeping others pure. It is the dogma that one race has carried progress with it throughout human history and can alone ensure future progress. It is a dogma rampant in the world today and which a few years ago was made into a principal basis of German polity.

Racism is not, like race, a subject the content of which can be scientifically investigated. It is, like a religion, a belief which can be studied only historically. Like any belief which goes beyond scientific knowledge, it can be judged only by its fruits and by its votaries and its ulterior purposes. Of course, when it makes use of facts, racist interpretation can be checked against those facts, and the interpretation can be shown to be justified or unjustified on the basis of history and of scientific knowledge such as we have reviewed in previous chapters. But the literature of racism is extraordinarily inept and contradictory in its use of facts. Any scientist can disprove all its facts and still leave the *belief* untouched. Racism, therefore, like any dogma that cannot be scientifically demonstrated, must be studied historically. We must investigate the conditions under which it arises and the uses to which it has been put.

E

Racism is essentially a pretentious way of saying that "I" belong to the Best People. For such a conviction it is the most gratifying formula that has ever been discovered, for neither my own unworthiness nor the accusations of others can ever dislodge me from my position—a position which was determined in the womb of my mother at conception. It avoids all embarrassing questions about my conduct of life and nullifies all embarrassing claims by "inferior" groups about their own achievements and ethical standards.

It has also the advantage of great simplicity. It avoids any of the actual complexities of human nature and of human history and sets up a five-word proposition which the most uneducated can remember and glory in: "I belong to the Elect." For political purposes the racist formula has no rival.

This formula in its modern guise would have been impossible before the days of Darwin and of anthropomorphic measurements. It appeals to evolution and to anthropometry. It claims that the Elect to whom I racially belong are *biologically* destined to lead human destiny, and that in destroying others they achieve the survival of the fittest. These Elect, moreover, can be identified by measurements of the body. These refinements could not have arisen in the world before the nineteenth century. Nevertheless the natural history of racism did not begin with this elaborated dogma.

Prehistory of Racism.

The formula "I belong to the Elect" has a far longer history than has modern racism. These are fighting words among the simplest naked savages. Among them this formula is an integral part of their whole life-experience, which is, from our point of view, incredibly limited. They may place the Creation of Man in the days of their father's great-grandfather; they may bound the world by a sea ten miles to the west and a range of hills twenty miles to the east. Whatever was outside this tiny territory, before the restless White people came, was as alien to them as the surface of Mars; they did not dream of man's long history on the earth. Their own little group, in this tiny corner of the world, lived and worked together, and in most tribes what benefited one benefited all; and their name in their own language for this tiny tribe was grandiloquently "The Human Beings," "Men." The designation applied only to their tiny group. Other peoples, the not-human, were fair game: they might be hunted like animals. They were not people with whom my own tribe had common cause: God did not create them of the same clay, or they did not spring out of the same water-jar, or they did not come up through the same hole in the ground. But my own little group was under the special providence of God; he gave it the middle place in the "world," and he foretold that, if ever it was wiped out, the world would perish. To my tribe alone he gave the ceremonies which preserve the world.

Such a world-view in a small, primitive tribe is not inconsistent with its experience. The tribe asks nothing from any other group; it supports itself adequately in isolation, and anything it can take from other people is clear gain. Even where primitive tribes include many thousands of people and occupy large territories, the picture usually does not differ essentially; the "in-group" —the tribal unit within which benefits are shared and activities carried out in common and where I behave with a certain ethical restraint toward my neighbours— this in-group knows its own worth and claims unique importance.

Such a primitive in-group is not a race, not even a small local sub-race or breed. The smallest racial unit is usually split up into many mutually death-dealing in-groups. Their antagonism is not racial but cultural. They do not keep their "blood" separate; each tribe may have made a practice of raiding for women in the other group, and their ancestry therefore may be traceable to the despised group almost in the same proportion as to its own vaunted one. Or recurrent peacemaking between them may be signalized by intermarriage, or marriages may be consummated for economic and social advantages. These practices occur whether the neighbouring tribes are of one breed or whether they belonged at some period to two which can be distinguished by different anthropomorphic measurements. The duty to keep the "blood" unmixed is a refinement based on so-called science.

This primitive in-group, dealing death to outsiders and furnishing mutual support to insiders, yet often taking wives from its enemies, easily became, even in many primitive regions of the world, an overlord tribe taking tribute or consolidating a larger empire. Even the conquests of Alexander the Great were fundamentally like those among many primitive African tribes. Aristotle was Alexander's mentor and he wrote out in his *Politics* (Chapter VII) the reasons why the fair-skinned barbarians and the Asiatic peoples could never rise to the level of the Greeks. His argument was the same as that of a Zulu of South Africa talking about the Bathonga: Was it not obvious that the foreigners' cultural attainments were inferior? Because he was not making a racist argument there was no reason why he should consider the attainments of Hellenized Asiatics; they were not pertinent to his argument because their attainments were high. Nor did he argue that Greek blood must be kept pure. His pupil Alexander, in the course of his conquests, advocated intermarriage, and ten thousand of his soldiers took wives from the natives of India. Alexander himself married two Persian princesses.

Aristotle's attitude was characteristic of Europe in ancient times, and the Roman Empire therefore did not have to free itself of racist doctrines in the building of its great cosmopolitan state. As Roman objectives became clearer and imperial edicts embodied these in law, the privileges of the capital city were more and more extended to the provinces. The Roman Empire was in many ways a new invention in human history, extending old in-group advantages over a great part of its enormous territory. Restrictions on trade and intercourse, which had earlier crippled each little separate district, were removed and large customs districts established, on the borders of which duties were levied for revenue only; and Rome reaped both prestige and profit from the rapid and progressive Latinization of its empire. An essential part of its administration was its consistent use of provincials in high office, where they were advanced according to ability. Provincials rose to high rank as soldiers, statesmen, and men of letters. The Roman legions were increasingly recruited from the provinces. From the first the highly prized prerogatives of Roman citizenship were extended to responsible persons of alien races. Paul's famous boast, made in the early years of the Empire, has brought this home to all readers of the New Testament: "But I am free (Roman) born"—that is, his father or his grandfather, Jews of the distant city of Tarsus, had been awarded Roman citizenship for their services or had bought it, like Paul's guard, "with a great price." Eventually the Roman franchise was extended to all inhabitants of the Empire who had not been born in slavery.

This lack of discrimination against aliens was not the result of specific ethical teaching, but of social forces which Roman administrative genius was able to use to its own profit. It was a tolerance which was compatible with imperialism as it was practised until very recent times. The principal objective of early imperialism was to secure tribute and to bind the subjugated areas to the capital, not, as in later forms, to exploit a new labour market in working mines or plantations. Therefore it was economical to honour the most able of the conquered peoples and depute authority to them. In regard to the folkways and cultural life of the provinces, Roman policy was one of *laissez faire*.

This attitude of the Roman Empire toward outsiders was historically an important step in widening the circle within which certain in-group prerogatives could be shared. An imperial peace was imposed over great areas of the world and a civil administration that looked to a common authority. Such social innovations had their repercussions in lessening the grandiose claims of each little local group and in breaking down the earlier barriers.

The Christian religion arose and spread in the same world that gave rise to the Roman Empire. Jesus taught the brotherhood of man. In Palestine in his day the alien was the hated Samaritan, and when the Samaritan woman said to him: "How is it that thou, being a Jew, askest drink of me, which am a woman of Samaria? For the Jews have no dealings with the Samaritans" (John iv, 9), he preached his gospel to her and her townsfolk and "many of them believed." His disciples were horrified, but at the end of his ministry they, too, believed that they were "to go into all the world and preach the gospel," and Paul, the most effective of these followers, taught that "there is neither Jew nor Greek, there is neither bond nor free, there is neither male nor female: for ye are all one in Christ Jesus" (Galatians iii, 28).

Such a programme and such a teaching were congruent with secular attitudes of the first-century Roman Empire as they had not been, for instance, in the times of Zoroaster, some thousand years earlier in Persia. Zoroaster had established a national cult that did not look beyond Persia; it was non-proselytizing, like a primitive religion. Confucius, too, in China in the era of rival overlords, left among his followers no idea of extending his teachings among all races of the world. The programme of Christianity, in its early growth, had behind it the secular idea of a larger community of all peoples such as the Roman Empire had been able to create.

The Hebrew law and the prophets also contributed to the foundations of Jesus's teaching. The ancient Mosaic law lays down gracious rules: "The stranger that dwelleth with you shall be unto you as one born among you, and thou shalt love him as thyself; for ye were strangers in the land of Egypt: I am the Lord your God" (Leviticus xix, 34). "One ordinance shall be both for you of the congregation, and also for the stranger that sojourneth with you, an ordinance for ever in your generations: as ye are, so shall the stranger be before the Lord" (Numbers xv, 15).

After the Assyrian captivity, however, an opposition party arose which advocated separatism. The prophet Ezra preached the abomination of mixing the seed of Israel with the seed of the Ammonite and the Moabite, and all wives and children of foreigners were deported and all future mixed marriages brought under a strong ban. Fanatical racism therefore occurred in Israel long before the days of modern racism, but no trace of it is to be found in the words of Christ. His teachings of a great community of peoples without regard to race agreed

with the older Hebraic law, and were given a solid basis,
also, by the achievements of the Roman Empire.

The Church of Rome, after Christianity became the
state religion, inherited both from imperial tradition and
from the teachings of Christ and his followers this belief
in the brotherhood of man without regard to race,
and acted upon it in its long overlordship of many
diverse nations and peoples in the Middle Ages. Even
today, in a world given over to racism, the Papacy
follows its long and honourable precedent and opposes
race prejudice in its pronouncements.

The social order in Europe changed radically in the
thirteenth century. That century marks the decay of
feudalism and the beginning of the decline of the secular
power of the Papacy. In long-range perspective, when
that century ended it carried with it the great institutions
of mediaeval times and was succeeded by those which
led up to the modern age.

Feudalism in the early Middle Ages had bound together
for certain mutual advantages all the ranks of society
from the highest to the lowest and placed upon all of
them mutual obligations of loyalty, protection, and
service. This condition was gradually altered; with
the collapse of feudalism serfs were no longer "tied to
the land," and were therefore no longer the responsibility
of their feudal lords. The security they had had was
one which gave them pitifully little of this world's goods,
but it offered at least a defence against utter destitution.
Like their lord's horses, they had been worth their
stabling; they could look to their overlord for a roof
and something to eat. Their new freedom was not much
more than the freedom to starve, and strife between the
classes became bitter and disastrous.

From the first beginnings of the modern age those
who held power in their hands had opportunity for

aggrandizement on a greater and greater scale. On the Continent local groups, when they were at least potentially equal, bled each other in a long series of mutual reprisals; when they conquered and could incorporate the new territory under their own authority these larger units matched themselves again with enemies of equal pretensions. The warring camps therefore grew from small local grand duchies to unified nations. Their one consistent policy has been to do to the other what the other would do to them, and to do it first. We are still in this era of international anarchy, though the warring groups have grown until they are in our century almost world-wide. Wars have been, and still are, disastrous just in proportion as the commercial and social interests of the warring camps have become actually more interdependent. This modern period from the thirteenth century to the present has been a struggle between warring camps in a civilization which, even as early as the period of the Roman Empire, had been administered as one, and as late as the Middle Ages had looked to one Universal Church which exercised both secular and religious authority. In the modern world the animosities and punitive policies of each group have become not only life-and-death threats to its neighbours but suicidal to itself. In such a world doctrines of the brotherhood of man have lost what basis in experience they had had in earlier times.

The modern world from its earliest days, therefore, has been an uncongenial home for the doctrine that God had made of one clay all the peoples of the earth. The warring and competing groups into which this world had for the time being resolved itself, whether they were nations or classes, had little experience on which to base a belief in the brotherhood of man; they needed instead a doctrine which taught that in the struggle of rival interests, which was the rule of the day, their favoured group was made of special clay.

Racism and European Expansion Overseas.

An occurrence, unprecedented in history, contributed to this separatism at the very beginning of modern times: the discovery of the New World and the exploitation and settlement of hitherto unknown islands and continents that followed. All Europe was excited by the discovery of so populous a world inhabited by so many different races. The excitement often took romantic forms in the stay-at-homes safe in the capitals of Europe who read with delight fanciful tales of the noble Red Man like Chateaubriand's *Atala* and *Paul et Virginie* and *Les Natchez*. Chateaubriand, it is admitted today, had never himself lived among the Indians; he had therefore not been imbued with frontier attitudes toward the savage. For, however stay-at-homes glorified "natives," frontiersmen and plantation-owners and slave-traders knew their place. Europeans overseas were waging an implacable war of extermination and subjugation. There were differences in the attitudes that settlers of different nations took toward the alien natives, and the Spanish and Portuguese and Dutch did not share the horror of miscegenation the English had, nor did the French institute the ironclad caste distinctions the English did. Frontiersmen of whatever nation, nevertheless, were out to gain their ends by whatever means, and none of them dealt with natives according to the cultural *laissez faire* of the Roman Empire.

In tropical countries Europeans wanted cheap labour and markets and slaves; in temperate countries they wanted the land to occupy as settlers. Wherever they went, Europeans were bent on extirpating the native religions. The natives were regarded as outside the pale of humanity, without religion, law, or morals. Bounties were placed on their heads, and they could be freely kidnapped or massacred. They had no redress but to strike back and so to bring upon themselves merciless reprisals. Even these presently became impossible, and the native remnants were herded onto reserves or became hopeless slaves in the mines or on the plantations. Those natives were alone fortunate who lived in countries that could not readily be exploited by Europe's traders or settled by her colonists.

The dogma of racial superiority and inferiority, however, even under these drastic conditions, did not arise for more than three centuries. Natives were outside the pale of humanity, but this was regarded as a consequence of the fact that they were not Christians, not of the fact that they belonged to the darker races. Religious persecution was the old familiar idea of the Middle Ages which had always been invoked against heretics and against Jews; racism had not yet appeared on the horizon. Like the Moslem today, the early European settlers divided mankind into the conquering "believer" and the victim "unbeliever." Even the slave-trade was originally justified on the grounds that the victims were lost souls and heathen. Of Prince Henry the Navigator it is said that "in pursuit of his crusading purpose he did not hesitate to sacrifice himself, and his zeal for religion led him to rejoice when a company of adventurers brought back cargoes of natives because of the salvation of those souls that before were lost." [1]

The "unbeliever" theory of native inferiority involved the Whites in many contradictions. In the early days the mere act of discovering a new part of the world

---

[1] Quoted in I. D. MacCrone, *Race Attitudes in South Africa*. London, 1937, p. 7.

was held to give that territory and its inhabitants to the European nation financing the expedition, but the duty of converting the natives to Christianity was a condition of this legal title.   Missionaries, often devoted and courageous, therefore accompanied every ship, especially those from the Catholic countries; and for the native who professed the faith the chasm that separated the white Christian from the coloured heathen was theoretically bridged.   This meant specifically that he could not be held in slavery, for the idea of a Christian slave was abhorrent in those times.   Henry the Navigator's long crusade against the Moors was waged to free their Christian slaves—to wipe out such an insult to Christendom.

The activities of missionaries, therefore, hampered the activities of exploiters and slave-traders; and, particularly in those countries overseas which were dominated by the Protestant nations of Europe, the practice of freeing slaves who professed Christianity gradually died out. In South Africa the Dutch, in order to avoid any question of emancipation, ruled that children born in slavery were neither to be baptized nor to be given religious instruction.   It was not till 1792 that the Church Council of Cape Town went on record with the statement that neither the law of the land nor the law of the Church ruled that Christian Negroes had to be freed; it added that in Cape Town many slaves were Christian.   By the beginning of the nineteenth century in South Africa, therefore, the old theory of a division of the human race into "believers" and "unbelievers" no longer corresponded to the facts, and the same dilemma was arising in other parts of the world.   Sometimes, as in South Africa, it arose in relation to slavery; and sometimes, as we read in old protests of Jesuit and Franciscan missionaries in the New World, in relation to massacres of Indian converts.   The time was ripe for a new theory of superiority and inferiority, and people began to talk of natives as sub-human, as related to apes rather than to civilized man. After all, colour was the most conspicuous difference, and it set off the opposing parties on the frontier as religion often no longer did. But the shift from one basis for the white man's superiority to the other was gradual and was not formulated. It was an inevitable response to social conditions and was practical rather than intellectualized. The situation on the frontier was a rough and ready one in which settlers and administrators acted according to the needs of the moment and did not generalize their difficulties into racist dogmas. They did not trouble themselves about cosmic justifications; it was quite enough for them that the natives were in the long run helpless before them.

In those overseas countries colonized by England the division into "believers" and "unbelievers" had, from the earliest times, a much less important place than it had in countries held by the nations of continental Europe. The English took from the first a highly secular attitude toward natives; in their administration the establishment of missions was not a regular part of claims to the territory; and if missions were established and natives converted, the difference between Christianized and non-Christianized natives was not officially important. The English dealt with natives as with a low, though sometimes useful, caste: they practised a rigid separatism. Whereas in the French, the Spanish, and the Portuguese colonies marriage with native women was common and a mixed population sprang up, in English colonies intermarriage was the great exception and there was strong feeling against it. In the colonization of that territory which is now the United States, therefore, the English frontiersman made a *racial* distinction; it was not phrased as such, however, because the fundamental conflict was a fight for land. The Englishman wanted the territories of the Indian, and he wanted them free of Indians. The early royal grants of land in the New World had made no mention of the natives already living there; they read as if no human being occupied the territories. The dearest wish of the settlers was to achieve this happy condition as soon as possible. They did not use the Indians in agricultural labour or in opening up the country as the Spanish did in Mexico; according to their scheme of things even that kind of contact with natives was too close: their one use of natives was as fighting allies against the French. In this they were singularly successful; their success in enlisting the Iroquois on their side against the French has often been declared decisive in preventing French expansion south of the St. Lawrence. When the wars were won, however, the aid they had rendered the English profited the Iroquois nothing. Again during the Revolution, and especially during the War of 1812, Indian tribes fought alongside their White allies. But the gulf was not to be bridged by such alliances. Those who fought on the side of the colonists and those who fought on the side of the British were equally stripped of their lands and herded onto reservations. In comparison with India and Africa, North America was very sparsely populated; and the English therefore could attain their prime object of separatism in a more drastic way than in the former countries where it had to be secured by caste distinctions. In America it was achieved by extermination and segregation. The conflict with the Indians remained a conflict for land and a series of reprisals; it was not ideological—not thought of, that is, as a "holy war" against a "tide of colour," nor were the Indians regarded as "the Mongol in our midst."

European expansion overseas, therefore, set the stage for racist dogmas and gave violent early expression to racial antipathies without propounding racism as a philosophy. Racism did not get its currency in modern thought until it was applied to conflicts within Europe— first to class conflicts and then to national. But it is possible to wonder whether the doctrine would have been proposed at all as explaining these latter conflicts— where, as we have seen, the dogma is so inept—if the basis for it had not been laid in the violent experience of racial prejudice on the frontier.

Racism and Class Conflicts.

Racism was first formulated in conflicts between classes. It was directed by the aristocrats against the populace. The first statement of the doctrine in modern Europe was directed against the monarchy also, since in France in 1727 the nobles felt themselves as much imposed upon by the king and his ministers as they were exasperated by the growing demands of the people. The Count de Boulainvilliers was a Norman with an extravagant admiration for the feudal system (already giving way to modern nationalism) and for the aristocrats who had been the feudal lords. He devoted himself to proving the pretensions of his family to membership in this ancient nobility. The feudal taxes that had been levied by the Crown, the arrogant authority of Louis XIV, roused in Boulainvilliers the dream that the nobles of his day would assert themselves against the State— *L'Etat, c'est moi*, Louis XIV had said—and re-establish their old glory. The wish was not new. In England under different circumstances it had led to the Magna Charta. But Boulainvilliers' procedure was quite different. He invoked racism. The nobles were the blood

of the *Germani*, the Teutonic barbarians who had overrun the Roman Empire and had been enthusiastically
described by the disaffected Roman moralist Tacitus
about A.D. 100. Tacitus, disgusted by what he considered the degeneracy of Rome—he wrote in the reign
of Trajan—extolled the hardihood and fierceness of the
barbarians and their "leadership principle": "Their
generals control them by example rather than by
authority. If they are daring and adventurous and
conspicuous in action, they procure obedience from
the admiration that they inspire." This aristocratic
freedom of the Teutonic tribes of the first century was,
according to Boulainvilliers' argument, the racial heritage
of the "Frankish" nobles of the eighteenth century, and
their blood demanded that they re-establish the aristocratic leadership that was theirs by blood. They must
end the absolute monarchy which stemmed from the
Roman idea of empire. The populace, on the other
hand, was of different clay; they were by race the old
conquered Gallo-Romans (Celts and Mediterraneans).
They were racially destined to inferior status just as the
nobles were to superior status.

The nobility, however, in spite of the Count's racist
argument, did not prove to have been eternally destined
to hold their ancient rank, and by the time of the French
Revolution in 1791 the "two Frances" into which
Boulainvilliers had divided the population had shifted
their relative positions. By that time spokesmen of the
populace could call the tune on the other side. The
Abbé Sieyès, for example, accepted the claims of the
nobles that they racially inherited the fruits of the
Frankish conquest. "Very well, we, the Gallo-Roman
plebs, will now conquer the nobility by expelling and
abolishing them. Our rights will supersede theirs on
exactly the principle they invoke." He was right; a less

pretentious statement of the fundamental racist dogmas is that nothing succeeds like success.

Racism, however, had no mass triumph in the days of the French Revolution. The great classic racist pronouncement was published in 1853-1857: Count de Gobineau's *Essay on the Inequality of Human Races*. Like Boulainvilliers, he taught that the hope of the world was and had always been the fair-haired Teutons, whom, according to the current fashion, he now called Aryan (today, read *Nordic*). But it was not a nationalist gospel he proclaimed. Gobineau, like Boulainvilliers, was French, and he was disgusted with political developments in France. He dedicated his two-volume essay to George V of Hanover, the blind German king who had just swept away the liberal constitution the people had compelled his father to grant, but Gobineau had no more faith in Germany's racial superiority than in that of France. Neither in France nor in Germany— nor in Scandinavia, when he visited Sweden—were there more than a handful of pure Aryans left: all European countries alike were swamped by the Gallo-Romans (today, read *Celt, Alpine, Mediterranean*). No European nation had enough racial aristocrats to base upon them any *national* claims to precedence. The Count de Gobineau wrote not as a modern nationalist, but, again like Boulainvilliers, as a conservative aristocrat. He was angered and disturbed by conditions which had just led up to the revolution of 1848. He had himself in that year been one of the founders of a *Revue* to work for the establishment of a republic led by aristocrats. There was widespread unemployment and great distress. Action was necessary. The socialist leaders succeeded in getting the principle of "the right to work" accepted, and a sort of WPA was established under the government. These were called "national workshops," and

they encountered the familiar trouble of our days; re-
munerative work could not be provided for all the
unemployed and doles had to be substituted. Even
these inadequate doles kept a horde of malcontents
dangerous to the government, and the whole arrangement was suddenly revoked. What followed were the
massacres of June—another struggle between the "haves"
and the "have-nots" at the barricades in the streets of
Paris.

It is the more necessary to root Gobineau's essay in
its historical background because he was not a closet
student nor an academician: he was a man of the
world whose stakes were in public life. He was during
his lifetime Cabinet Secretary, Minister to Persia, and
his government's representative on missions to Brazil
and many European capitals. He was a writer of novels,
plays, and travel books. He was caught up in a world
in which the unwashed mob were in despair and were
demanding some means to live. It could not be denied
them on the basis of Rousseau's Social Contract or even
of Hobbes's idea of the State; it could be denied them,
however, on the basis of congenital inferiority—that is,
on the basis of race. As he himself wrote, his object
was to fight well against the growing demands of the
under-privileged; he wanted to "do better than de
Maistre and de Bonald against liberalism." [1]

Therefore, dedicating his volume to George V of
Hanover, who had just had a similar conflict on his
hands, he wrote: "Gradually I have become convinced
that race overshadows all other problems in history, that
it holds the key to them all, and that the inequality of
people from whose fusion a people is formed is enough

[1] Letter to Probusch—Osten, June 10, 1856, quoted by Jacques Barzun
in *Race: a Study in Modern Superstition*. London, Methuen & Co., 1938,
p. 93, n. 5.

to explain the whole course of its destiny. I convinced myself at last that everything great, noble, and fruitful in the works of man on this earth, in science, art, and civilization, derives from a single starting point; it belongs to one family alone, the different branches of which have reigned in all the civilized countries of the universe." These aristocrats, who had reigned in all countries, were now threatened by the degeneracy of democracy and by claims of equality. When he divided the races of the world into White, Yellow, and Black, his application of the matter was that the Alpines were of Yellow extraction and the Mediterraneans of Black extraction; his Whites were represented, therefore, in Europe only by the group which is today called Nordic. They were the only ones on whom the hope of civilization could be pinned. They alone had "reflective energy," "perseverance," "instinct for order," "love of liberty," "honour." The loss of their position in Europe meant the twilight of civilization.

This gospel of Gobineau's has been distorted by his twentieth-century followers into a gospel of nationalism, and Germany today reads "modern Germans" wherever Gobineau wrote "Aryans"—this in spite of his insistence that his Aryans were no more common in Germany than elsewhere. His argument has been misread also by modern critics, who all read nationalism into his racial doctrines. They therefore point out absurdities and contradictions which stem from their own misunderstanding rather than from Gobineau's position. They make much of the fact that he insists over and over again that no civilization has been the work of a pure race, and nevertheless conclude that societies perish only because they have lost their pure and uncontaminated blood. This would have been a contradiction had he been writing a nationalist manifesto, but Gobineau was

defending the rôle of the aristocratic remnant endangered
by a bastard proletariat. His whole volume is an attempt
to prove that civilizations rise and fall along with the
fortunes of the conquering aristocracy, an aristocracy
which is defined by birth. When the aristocracy is lost
in the surrounding mob, the country is doomed.

Gobineau, therefore, accepts as the very basis of his
racist doctrines the fact that civilizations are all built on
a mixture of races. His Aryan race was a race of rulers,
and "every founder of a civilization would wish the
backbone of his society, his middle class, to consist of
Yellow races." (Alpines, numerically predominant in
France, he had defined as of Yellow extraction.) "It
would be unjust," he says, "to say that every mixture is
bad and harmful"; in fact, "from the point of view of
beauty" the finest racial blend "is the offspring of the
White and Black." (Gobineau had described Mediterraneans as Black. A Frenchman could talk of miscegenation between Black and White; an Anglo-Saxon
would hesitate to do so.)

The fact that all nations are a composite of races means
to Gobineau that they are stratified into classes and that
their glory depends upon only one of these classes. He
never preached the doctrine of pure race as the basis of
any civilization: "Aryans had ceased to be pure as
early as the birth of Christ." Nevertheless, his whole
argument depended, consistently enough from his point
of view, upon the fixity of racial type—in the individual,
not in the nation. It was the "nobility of our species"
(the Aryans) which was indestructible and which had
been transferred intact down the ages by heredity; their
racial type had not been affected by climate, country, or
lapse of time. Upon this depended the unbridgeable
chasm between the aristocrat and the populace, the importance in world history of the one and the negligibility

of the other. He wrote to make the aristocratic "Aryan" remnant conscious of its "mission" in the high purposes of civilization and to convince the non-Aryans that their sole duty was to respect this "mission."

Only as individuals could Gobineau hope to identify his "Aryan" supermen, individuals here and there who still held in their hands, by racial destiny, the hope of the world. But he knew that he himself belonged to this Elect. His *Essay on Human Inequality* was "written only to serve as preface" for his researches in his own family tree, researches which he published in 1879 as *The History of Ottar Jarl, Norwegian Pirate, Conqueror of Bray in Normandy, and of His Descendants*. It was a genealogy perhaps as well authenticated as most genealogies which go back to the Vikings, and it was a labour of love which freed him of his own prosperous bourgeois father and established him as one of his "race of princes." It was the racial ancestry of the chosen few in which he believed, not the pure ancestry of a nation.

Gobineau's *Essay* is still the classic document of racism, and its argument is so universally read today as nation-alistic propaganda that its place in history is misunder-stood. Gobineau was neither pro-French nor pro-German—in spite of the volumes his followers have written claiming the one or the other—he was pro-aristocracy. He hated patriotism, which he scorned as a Latin provincialism unworthy of his Elect. He wrote that nationalism had been the chief cause of French defeat in the War of 1870. He was, during his later years, unwaveringly anti-government, and for this reason French racialists today borrow from his arguments without acknowledging the source; they do not like the bitterness with which he described the conduct of France in the War of 1870. Gobineau's message was that of the incomparable worth of the patricians and their culture,

and his eyes were fastened on a lost golden age when
their worth had not been contested. He had the aristocrat's contempt for commerce—which was due to the
"poison of racial intermixture"—and for the techno-
logical inventions of modern civilization; printing,
steam power, and industrial discoveries, he wrote, were
mere matters of routine which "Aryans" would not
have concerned themselves with. He left them to the
mob.

Gobineau wrote in the early 1850's, when anthropomorphic measurements were few and uncritical and
before Darwin had published the *Origin of Species*. He
could not foresee the distribution of racial traits as they
are known today and he could not foresee the laws of
genetics. After Darwin the "survival of the fittest" was
added to racist pronouncements, but Gobineau had
pictured his Aryans rather as fine flowers of mankind
and had often endowed them with the more fragile
virtues.

His successors have developed his doctrines, therefore,
along two lines: first, the interpretation of anthropometric measurements, and, second, the "survival of the
fittest." Because of this latter borrowing from Darwinism, racist theories after Gobineau gave more and more
weight to the sacredness of conquest and of force. Conquerors—who might be pictured either as a privileged
nobility or as a nation embracing all classes—had
succeeded because they were by nature the fittest; a
"scientific" reason had been discovered which sanctified
the old axiom that might makes right.

Another development of racism, that based on anthropometric measurements, was pushed vigorously in France
during the latter half of the nineteenth century. Broca,
Lapouge, and Ammon in Germany are the names that
stand out in the energetic school that called itself an-

thropo-sociology. In contrast to the romantic Gobineau, they were prodigious collectors of measurements, avid statistical students, and they sought to find the answers to specific rather than to cosmic problems. Nevertheless, they were truly of the Boulainvilliers-Gobineau school of racists in that they, too, did not make nationalistic application of their material; they were concerned with class differences. They investigated the "two Frances" and the "two Germanies," the narrow-headed Nordics and the broad-headed Alpines; and their Elect were, as with the earlier racists, the Nordic narrow-heads. Their problem was to determine the inferiority or superiority of different strains within Western Europe. The lack of nationalism in their position even allowed this school to work in harmony on both sides of the Rhine: Ammon's work was done in Germany (Baden), and Broca's and Lapouge's in France.

They all used mass anthropomorphic measurements to show that the narrow-heads (Nordics) were the adventurous, aggressive race, and the broad-heads (Alpines) the timid, submissive subject race. In Lapouge's figure of speech the narrow-heads are the hunting pack and the broad-heads the marauded sheep. In line with the sacred "survival of the fittest," which the school owed to Darwin, the Elect was clearly the hunting pack. Of course, skull measurements of European populations do not of themselves separate the hunting pack from the sheep, but a test case was propounded: Since cities are "advanced" as compared with rural populations, the Elect should be concentrated in the cities. This was indeed a fact which had been noted in south-central France, in northern Italy, and in Germany before the rise of the anthropo-sociological school, and in its earlier, more aristocratic form—nobles, instead of city dwellers —it had been recognized by Gobineau. Ammon inter-

preted this difference in average head form in city and
country as evidence of social selection; the higher
average of narrow-heads in the cities showed that their
abilities were greater and had been " selected." "Social
selection" he placed in the same position in human
history as Darwin had placed "natural selection" in
animal history. This urban concentration of long-heads
to the disadvantage of broad-heads is known as Ammon's
law, and was interpreted as proving the racial superiority
of long-heads.

Had it not been for the racist traditions and the
hallowed claims of the fair, blue-eyed narrow-heads, the
facts could have been interpreted, by the same arguments
this school advanced, as proving the exact opposite.
For their data all showed that the cephalic index was
increasing—that is, that narrow-heads were losing out
to round-heads. Also complexions were growing darker.
Since population was increasing more rapidly in cities
than in the country, these changes were the more marked
in the cities. Why not a social selection of round-heads?
The anthropo-sociological school confined itself to the
statistics of cephalic indices and in no case set itself the
task of showing that broad-heads were inferior in length
of life or fertility.

It is unnecessary to choose between one interpretation
of these facts and the other, for the universality of the
facts themselves was soon disproved. Livi[1] in his military
statistics of Italy showed that in some districts, like Pied-
mont, the city population was on the average more long-
headed than that of the surrounding district, just as in
Germany, but that in other districts, like Palermo, it
was the other way round. The explanation was simple:
the city population was drawn from a wider area than
the rural population and, therefore, whether the latter

[1] Livi, *Anthropometria militaire*. Rome, 1896.

was long- or short-headed, differed from it. The inferiority or superiority of the strains was in no way involved.

The figures accumulated by the school of anthroposociology are more striking in their overlapping than in their significant differences. Both city-born and country-born have the same range; there are a few *more* narrow-heads than broad-heads in the cities, and that is all. To speak of "concentration of narrow-heads" in the cities, when the cephalic index of Heidelberg students from the the country averaged 82·7 and from the city 81, is to mistake the situation. All the measurements established the fact that the same *range* of cephalic indices was found in the city and in the country; even if one could grant that all city dwellers were congenitally superior to all country dwellers, city people did not most of them have long heads.

The whole racist argument of the school of anthroposociology seems pretentious and distorted to modern investigators, and their sole reliance on the cephalic index is regarded as thoroughly unsatisfactory. The importance of this school in the history of racist dogmas is that it reflected changing conditions in Europe. It was still pre-nationalistic, and in no way anticipated the twentieth-century patriotic pronouncements; the problem it posed was a class problem of inferiority or superiority of different strata within the nation. But instead of seeing the problem in terms of feudalism or the well-born as Boulainvilliers and Gobineau had seen it, the students of 1850-1900 saw it in terms of urban prestige. They could, of course, have measured descendants of the nobility and compared them with the bourgeoisie or the peasants, and if conditions had been what they were in earlier generations they would no doubt have done so. In an urban age they arranged their material to show the characteristics of city dwellers and to argue from these traits their innate superiority.

Racism, the doctrine of the innate superiority of a class, became in Europe, about the time of the turn of the century, a doctrine of the superiority of nations; but in America it has maintained its earlier meaning. This is a reflection at once of the lesser menace of other armed nations in the New World and of the recency and the proportions of immigrations which have brought representatives of all European ethnic groups in great numbers to the United States. About 1890 the immigrants, who since the earliest colonization had been drawn from Northern and Western Europe, began to come, as a result of European conditions, chiefly from Southern and Eastern Europe. The racist literature which this called forth asserts the superiority of the Nordics and the inferiority of the non-Nordics, and derives from this that the United States is in danger because the blood of her older settlers is being contaminated by mixture with that of the later comers. The difficulties of the post-war years were ascribed *en masse* to the immigration policy the United States had pursued and to the groups that had most recently taken advantage of it. These immigrants were obviously poverty-stricken and employed mainly as unskilled labour. As a group they made a poor showing beside the immigrants who had settled in this country before 1890. The American racists cut, at one stroke, the Gordian knot of historical and sociological facts and ascribed the obvious condition of the Italian and Polish immigrant to his innate inferiority as a non-Nordic.

The arguments the American racists presented to uphold this interpretation were taken from Gobineau and Houston Chamberlain. In Europe, according to Madison Grant, "the amount of Nordic blood in each nation is a very fair measure of its strength in war and standing in civilization," [1] but his application of this principle would not recommend itself to German and French racialists. "The Germans of today are for the most part descendants of the peasants"—the author's alternative designation of the Alpine broad-heads—and this explains the present "ghastly rarity in the German armies of chivalry and generosity toward women and of knightly protection and courtesy toward the prisoners or wounded." [2]   France has been ruined in the same manner: "Step by step, with the reappearance of these primitive and deep-rooted stocks [Alpine and Medi-terranean] the Nordic element in France declined, and with it the vigour of the nation." [3] The same substitution of one race for another accounts for "the superstitious and unintelligent Spaniard of today."   In England, too, the Nordics are receding. This desperate state of affairs in Europe, however, since *The Passing of the Great Race* is written by an American, leads in its author's view to glorious prospects for the United States if the older immigrants keep their dominant position. For down to the time of the Civil War the White race in our country was "purely Nordic . . . not only Nordic but also purely Teutonic, a very large majority being Anglo-Saxon in the most limited meaning of that term." [4]   Even at the date of writing he announces that the majority of Ameri-cans are Nordic. All that is needed in order that the United States shall take the glorious position Europe has lost is, in the words of Henry Fairfield Osborn in his Introduction to Grant's book, to combat "the gradual dying out among our people of those hereditary traits through which the principles of our religious, political or

---

[1] Grant, Madison, *The Passing of the Great Race*. London, G. Bell & Sons, 1917, p. 175.
[2] *Ibid.*, pp. 167-168.   [3] *Ibid.*, p. 177.   [4] *Ibid.*, pp. 72-74.

social foundations were laid down, and their insidious replacement by traits of less noble character." [1] In later racist books in America, Nordic racial hygiene, the obligation of the chosen race to keep its blood free from contamination with that of lesser breeds, was raised to the pinnacle of patriotic duty.

The application of these time-worn doctrines to America was inept in the extreme. The gratuitous assumption of the superiority of the Nordic in Europe we have already examined in considering the racist volumes written in Europe. Grant merely repeated these claims. The identification of all older American immigrants as Nordic, however, was a contention not advanced among European racists. Grant arrived at it not by use of any anthropomorphic measurements, but by the perusal of lists of nationalities from which immigrants were drawn before 1860. He himself made the point that Great Britain and Germany, the two chief sources of this immigration, were at that time losing or had already lost their Nordic pre-eminence. Hence it would seem necessary for him to have proved that some factors had caused a *racial* selection of Nordic elements in these populations and had left behind the non-Nordic. This he failed to do. Actually, whatever selection occurred, it did not operate to make English blonds emigrate and English brunettes stay in Europe. The motive was generally economic and operated in the same manner for blonds and brunettes.

An anthropomorphic analysis of "Old Americans" has been made by Aleš Hrdlička [2] which shows clearly the fallacy of Grant's supposition. This study examines two thousand Americans whose four grandparents were all born on American soil. "Light" hair colour was found in only 5·3 per cent. of these Old Americans, "light brown" in only 16 per cent. In hair colour, skin colour,

[1] *Ibid.*, p. ix.   [2] Hrdlička, Aleš, *Old Americans*. Baltimore, 1925.

and eye colour 75 per cent. were "medium" or "dark." As Huxley and Haddon say: "The study of Dr. Hrdlička's work will leave little doubt that . . . the Nordic element in the 'Old American' is small." [1]

In all the American racist volumes there was an immediate political objective: revision of the immigration laws. The American temper had changed since the days when our motto was "No distinctions of race, creed, or colour," and we offered an "asylum for the oppressed" and wrote enthusiastically about "the Melting Pot." It was becoming harder to offer opportunity to all Americans, and the social engineering that America needed was to be had only at a price. Because of social conditions in the United States there was no doubt that immigration could no longer be left wide open. The only point at issue was the basis on which choice should be made. Grant's *The Passing of the Great Race* was written in 1916, and by 1921 a hurried piece of legislation, the Quota Act, was rushed through Congress to check the rapid increase of immigration that followed the World War. Subsequent acts have modified percentages and changed the dates used for reckoning quotas, but they have followed the original principle. This principle was to admit new immigrants in numbers calculated at a certain percentage—3 per cent. in 1921, 2 per cent. in 1924—of the American foreign-born at certain dates—1910 in the Act of 1921, 1890 in the Act of 1924. The total number admitted in any year was fixed in 1924 at 150,000. In 1929 the "National Origin" provision, which depends on a more complicated calculation, went into effect. Immigrants from independent countries of the Americas and those from Canada are exempt from quota restrictions.

[1] Huxley, J. S., and Haddon, A. C., *We Europeans*. London, Jonathan Cape, 1935, p. 157.

If American thinking had not been confused by racist dogmas, the immigration regulations might have been drawn up on a socially more advantageous basis. Health and education are not determined by "national origins"; they are individual. In view of the cost of assimilating non-English-speaking, cheap-labour groups we might have announced frankly our preference for the educated. We might have chosen to admit emigrants from countries whose social order and standard of living are comparable to our own. Principally, however, the fixed annual number admitted was a shot in the dark. With every change in the economic condition of America the social advantage or disadvantage of additional man-power varies. During the depression of the last decade the Immigration Service has actually tried to balance man-power and employment by free interpretation of the phrase "liable to become a public charge." Adjustment to economic conditions in America has, however, been left to administrative interpretation; it has never been recognized in the law of the land or placed in the hands of a fact-finding commission.[1]

The racist literature of the United States [2] deals hardly at all with our great national racial problem, the Negro. Our treatment of the Negro conforms so closely to the predilections of these authors that they doubtless had little to suggest. On the other hand, they made the most of the opportunity to seize upon a racial basis to differentiate the still unassimilated labourer from the earlier and now more prosperous settlers. Their constant in-

---

[1] For an excellent discussion of the problems of minority groups, see Young, Donald, *American Minority Peoples*. London, Harper, 1932.

[2] Grant, Madison, *The Passing of the Great Race*, London, G. Bell & Sons, 1917. Burr, Clinton Stoddard, *America's Race Heritage*, New York, 1922. Stoddard, Lothrop, *The Revolt Against Civilization; the Menace of the Under Man*, London, Chapman & Hall, 1922. Gould, Charles W., *America : a Family Matter*, New York, 1 922. Osborn, Henry Fairfield, *Man Rises to Parnassus*, London, Oxford University Press, 1928.

junction is that Old America should limit immigration on a "racial" basis and should keep its blood free from mixture with that of the inferior non-Nordics we have carelessly admitted. Racism in America turned out to be no more than a spectacle of immigrants of one decade condemning to everlasting inferiority the immigrants of a later decade. It is the part of wisdom to wait a little longer before we commit ourselves to such judgments. A Norman in the time of Ivanhoe could have written of the impossibility of civilizing the Saxons with much better justification than does Madison Grant of non-Nordics in the 1920's in America, but to what purpose? History has long since reversed such a judgment, and to Madison Grant himself to be an Anglo-Saxon is the proudest boast. Americans of the future may likewise boast of heritages that today appear no more promising than that of Anglo-Saxon seemed not so long ago to the Norman.

Racism and Nationalism.

By the beginning of the twentieth century the nations of Europe were drawn up against each other in increasingly bitter conflict. Nationalism was the juggernaut before which all lesser causes became unimportant. Class rivalries and minority conflicts were crushed before it at every crisis. When in the 1890's Gobineau's *Essay* was resuscitated from comparative oblivion and its dogmas passionately and popularly espoused, it was not as a gospel of class but as a gospel of national patriotism. If pure racial heredity for a class in modern Europe or America was an impossible claim, pure racial heredity for a nation was a fantastic one. With European rules of property entailed in the family line, the privileged classes had a certain family continuity at least in one male line, and in spite of the fact that *any* ancestor is as important in the eyes of the biologist as the one who gives the surname, nevertheless this lent a certain verisimilitude to hereditary claims of the individual. With a nation, however, the verisimilitude vanishes. The popularizing of the doctrine had nevertheless been made easier both by increasing familiarity with the slogans when they were still class doctrines and by the uncritical notion that every group that differed was a "race." If Frenchmen and Germans differed, by that token they were different races.

Racism became a national battle-cry in this era of nationalism. In "fatherlands" in need of a common rallying-cry it provided a pedigree and a bond any man could understand and take pride in. Racism therefore became a babel of voices. The French, the Germans, the Slavs, the Anglo-Saxons—each produced their literary and their political spokesmen proving that to their "race" alone from the beginning of European history the triumphs of civilization had been due. Each laid violent hands on the facts of race and distorted them to contrary racist conclusions. Racism in its national phase lost any pretence of scientific objectivity.

There had been, of course, patriotic racist pronouncements almost from the time of Darwin. But they were scattered and casual. The first wave of national racism occurred, significantly enough, in France immediately after her defeat and humiliation by Germany in 1870. German armies had invaded France and taken Paris, and along with that triumph Bismarck had succeeded in unifying the kingdoms and grand duchies west of the Rhine into the unified German nation. France had for the time being lost her place as a great European power; and internal conflicts, which had weighed so heavily with Gobineau, were overshadowed by a humiliation the whole nation had experienced together. The new character of the groups in conflict immediately brought forth its counterpart: a change in racist theories. Gobineau's exaltation of the Aryans (Teutons) had given an equal place in the sun to both France and Germany, whether defeated or victorious, if they kept pure their fair, long-headed supermen. The French of 1871 found this pronouncement unsatisfactory, and they were not long in remedying it. Quatrefages, the Director of the National History Museum in Paris, published *La Race Prussiene*,[1] in which he singled out Bismarck's conquering kingdom of Prussia and provided it with a racial ancestry entirely distinct from that of France. The inhabitants of Prussia, wrote Quatrefages, were not Aryans at all. To judge of their race one must study the Finns, that tall, fair, broad-headed race to the north of Prussia. The Finns had mixed with Slavs, representatives of the old Asiatic invaders of Europe, and it was this race which inhabited the whole of Prussia. In overrunning the high civilization of France they were but once more the scourge of Europe.

The racial gulf between France and Germany was argued also in a quite different fashion. The dean of anthropometric scholars in France, the indefatigable Broca, published five volumes [2] containing the skull measurements of both living and dead, and showing— what was already well known—the numerical predominance of broad-heads in France. France, Broca proclaimed, was a nation of Gallic (read *Alpine*, *Celtic*) broad-heads, and he reversed Gobineau's pronouncement of their inferiority. The broad-heads, he stated, had undoubtedly larger and better brains than the long-heads. Thus the

---

[1] English translation: Quatrefages, Jean-Louis Armand de, *The Prussian Race*, London, 1872. Translated by Isabella Innes.
[2] Broca, Paul, *Mémoires d'Anthropologie*. Paris, 1871.

F

Germans might pride themselves on their Nordic blood, but the French should· pride themselves on their Gallic blood. The difficulty, which Broca's theory of French Gallicism did nothing to remove, is that the Germans are also predominantly broad-headed.

Both Broca and Quatrefages were pioneers in accurate anthropometric measurement of great populations, and they contributed much to our knowledge of European physical types. In a fashion unknown to Gobineau they used actual measurements in their arguments. Their researches on *race* advanced knowledge; the racist conclusions they drew were a quite different matter. All objective investigation indicates that an equally good brain can be housed in a broad or a long skull case, and, besides, the distribution of these physical types is quite similar in Germany and in France. On these precarious foundations, however, a chasm was fixed between the hated enemy and their own suffering nation. The racist theories of Broca and Quatrefages showed, not for the last time, how race data can be interpreted according to the pressing political needs of the moment.

Broca's exaltation of the broad-heads became the popular watchword of France during the whole lifetime of the "generation of 1870." In art and literary criticism, in political pronouncements, the cult of Celticism (read *Gallic, Alpine*) became a mystic faith. Under its favoured designation of Celticism it allowed for racial ties with England, then growing in popularity in France, and dug deeper the channels of France's eastern barrier, the Rhine. Historians joined also; .the dean of French historians, Fustel de Coulanges, proved that Germanic influences had had no part in forming the civilization of France.

On the other side of the Rhine the Germans were not slow to adopt their own racial theories. They had no

need, as the French had, to change Gobineau's categories, and it was Germany which first made his work
politically important. Richard Wagner, in his rôle as
a passionate German nationalist, found the Count's
Essay after his own heart and provided means for popularizing his writings in Germany. It was not until after
Gobineau's death, however, that the *Gobineau Vereinigung*
was founded in Germany in 1894, and not until 1899
that Wagner's son-in-law, Houston Chamberlain, one of
Gobineau's earlier youthful disciples, published *Foundations of the Nineteenth Century* [1]—a work that made Gobinism
a paramount cult in Germany.

The two bulky volumes of the *Foundations* seem today
among the most confused, pretentious, and overwritten
books that racism has produced, but they were welcomed
in Germany with signal honours. The Kaiser read them
aloud to his sons, had them distributed to officers of the
Army, and directed that they be displayed in libraries
and book-shops throughout Germany. The work went
through edition after edition. Its contentions became
part of the folk-thought of the German nation.

The *Foundations* criticizes Gobineau severely, yet the
racist position is much the same in the two authors.
The situation to which racist theories had to be applied,
however, had changed, and this led, as it always has in
the history of racism, to new identifications of ancient
and modern "races." The early Germanic tribes,
which represented the superman to Gobineau, had left
their heirs, he believed, among the aristocracy of many
European nations; these same early Germanic tribes
were, for Chamberlain, on the other hand, the settlers
and defenders of the nation now united under the name

---

[1] Chamberlain, Houston Stewart, *Die Grundlagen des neunzehnten Jahrhunderts*, Munich, 1899. English translation : *The Foundations of the Nineteenth Century*, London, 1911, 2 vols. : Translated by John Lees.

of Germany. He called them the Teutons, but they were not merely the blond, long-headed Nordics; if they had been, the German nation could not be as a whole the heirs of these predestined conquerors. Germans are, it is well known, some of them blond, some brunette, some long-headed, and some—the majority—broad-headed. Chamberlain's "Teutons," therefore, are not blond and long-headed, nor dark and short-headed: they are both. Measurements of skull or tabulation of hair colour were not called for in his scheme. "Teutons" were not merely the early Germanic tribes Tacitus had described; they were Celts and Slavs as well. "The Celts, Slavs, and Teutons are descended from a single pure stock," [1] and therefore any triumph of the Teutons proper is a triumph for all the Chosen People. In this way Chamberlain reworked Gobineau's racist theories so that no German need be excluded. He fitted his praise to the German nation, and in that nation he found this blood of the Chosen People in its greatest purity. Mixture of blood among his three chosen stocks had prevented sterility and made for German greatness.

If physical characteristics do not identify Chamberlain's Great Race, upon what does he rely? This Race alone understands the Principle of Leadership; it gives unfaltering loyalty to the leader of its choice. If he finds this trait among Italians or Frenchmen, he discovers them, too, to be Teutons in whatever country they were born. Their presence in these other countries only proved to Chamberlain that what greatness these nations had achieved was due to German blood; he claimed as Teutons Louis XIV, Dante, Michelangelo, Marco Polo, and Jesus Christ. His great concern was to define race so that it could rule out no member of the German nation: "Whoever reveals himself German by his acts,

[1] *Ibid.*, Vol. I, p. 499, note.

whatever his genealogical tree, is a German." In these pronouncements *race* ceases to have any assignable meaning, but such is obviously the price that must be paid for trying to draw up racist theories that can be applied to the mongrel nations of Europe in the twentieth century. In Chamberlain, this Nemesis overtook the gospel of racism.

He expounded anti-Semitism in the same manner. The *Foundations* stated all the racist pronouncements against the Jews which, in the past decade, we have come to associate with the Third Reich. Chamberlain, however, did not distinguish Semites by physical traits or by genealogy; Jews, as he knew, cannot be accurately separated from the rest of the population in modern Europe by tabulated anthropomorphic measurements. But they were enemies because they had special ways of thinking and acting. "One can very soon become a Jew . . . it needs only to have frequent intercourse with Jews, to read Jewish newspapers, etc." [1] Chamberlain is therefore the most frank of the pre-War racists. Carrying out their arguments to their necessary conclusions, he disavows race completely and boasts that it is irrelevant to the racist position. Post-War racists have repeated Chamberlain's self-contradiction whenever it was to their advantage to do so.

Racist literature in Germany became more and more inspirational, less and less hampered by facts as the World War drew near, and by 1914 racism had become a nationalistic faith. After the World War and the fall of the Weimar Republic, a defeated and disrupted Germany made racism the basis of national policy. It was not so difficult as it might seem to change the German racist theories from the boast of all-conquerors to the uses of a humiliated and despairing people. When

[1] *Ibid.*, Vol. I, p. 491.

Hitler wrote *Mein Kampf* in prison in the 1920's, he indicated the line along which this transformation was to be accomplished. Pre-War Germany had ignored the racial basis of nationality, "the one and only law which makes life possible on this earth"; it had nurtured the viper Judaism in its bosom, and the Jews had been responsible for national defeat. Therefore the whole involved problem of who was Nordic, who Slav, and who Alpine in Germany was politically irrelevant; the enemy was the Jew and the Jew could be identified through his genealogy. For difficult cases Nazi theory still fell back on Chamberlain's pronouncement that a man might be a true German without a German genealogy; they called it "a German soul in a non-German body." But this evasion was saved for exceptional cases. The basis of racism in all other cases was genealogy—a genealogy in which there was no Jewish parent or grandparent. In this form racism became the basis of National Socialism. The programme was stated in 1920 in the first draft of the Nazi programme by the then unknown party leaders headed by Adolf Hitler, and included: Citizenship and public office are possible only to those of German blood (i.e. to none with Jewish blood); non-citizens are to be deported if any true Germans are unemployed, and in any case are to remain in Germany only as guests under special laws; immigration of all with alien blood to be prohibited, etc. etc.

Immediately upon Hitler's assumption of power in 1933 laws began to be passed putting into effect different items of this programme, and scattered anti-Semitic persecutions soon occurred. It was not until the autumn of 1935, however, that the comprehensive rulings known as the Nuremberg Laws deprived all Jews of the right of citizenship, prohibited marriages between Jews and German non-Jews, and made a criminal offence of extramarital relations between them. In the same month all Jewish children were removed from the elementary schools. A year later the expropriation, without recompense, of Jewish property and banking accounts was begun, and in 1937 this was systematically prosecuted with the object of eliminating Jews from trade and commerce. In 1938 outbursts against the Jews became general, and mass arrests took place in Berlin. All the world knows the pogroms that simultaneously occurred throughout Germany on November 10 of that year, and the edict which made all damage done during these outbreaks collectable claims against the Jews, plus a fine upon them of one billion marks. By this time the emigration of helpless and poverty-stricken Jews from Germany and Austria had become an international problem, and early in 1939 the Jewish community in Berlin received orders from the police to produce daily the names of one hundred Jews, who would then receive two weeks' notice to leave the country. No provisions were made to finance this emigration. In Nazi-dominated parts of Europe the doctrines of racism had borne their bitter fruit.

Racism in the Third Reich, however, is not only a matter of anti-Semitism. From the first it involved also a programme of Pan-Germanism—"Union," as the 1920 platform stated, "of all Germans in a Greater Germany." Germans lived not only in Germany and Austria; there were thirty million scattered throughout the world. They were "as good as we are," and they were by the ineradicable fact of blood members of the German nation. There are some seven million German Americans, and any of these—or any Germans living under other governments—were branded as traitors if they assisted "opponents of the Third Reich," among whom the Nazis have long counted the United States.

Racism in the Third Reich has been altered to meet each new wind of political expediency. Chamberlain held that the Teuton was racially Christian, and he heaped panegyrics upon Christianity; Alfred Rosenberg, editor-in-chief of official newspapers and specifically in charge of racial indoctrination, pronounced the Christian church the chief menace to true Nordics, who will come into their own only when they have reasserted their old militant paganism and thrown off the Jewish Asiatic Catholic dominance to which they have been subjected in the Church.[1] He discovers a racial antipathy in the Nordics to the decadent words of the Sermon on the Mount.

Political developments, however, have led to even more fundamental changes in orthodox racism. Chamberlain, as we have seen, based the greatness of Germany on the intermixture by marriage of Teutons, Celts, and Slavs— all "descended from a single pure stock." But the Third Reich's holy opposition to Russian Communism from 1934 to 1939 made the Slavs unacceptable as members of the Chosen People. They became in Nazi propaganda enemies not only in ideology but congenitally by blood. This view was dropped even before the signing of the non-aggression pact in August 1939, and German silence on this score was one of the reasons on which some close observers based their belief that such a treaty was under consideration.

Germany's alliance with Italy raised a similar difficulty. Orthodox racism of the pre-War and World War period had been full of contempt for the Mediterranean race, but the Rome-Berlin Axis had to be given a racial basis. Much was made, therefore, of the German-ness of northern Italy and the fact that classic German racists

[1] Rosenberg, Alfred, *Der Mythus des Zwanzigsten Jahrhunderts*. Munich, 1935.

had ascribed all achievements beyond the Alps to in-
filtrations of northern blood; Chamberlain and others
had outdone themselves in claiming as "Nordics" such
Italians as Dante, Petrarch, Giotto, Leonardo, and
Michelangelo. The same Italy which in 1915 France
had welcomed as an ally because they both were racially
Latin, Germany now welcomed on the basis of their
common Teutonic blood.

The alliance with Japan was a more difficult matter.
Hitler excepts the Japanese when he strikes out at non-
Aryans, and Japanese residents of Germany are not
subject to the racial laws of the Third Reich. They may
therefore marry with German Aryans without polluting
the pure blood extolled by the Nazis. Hans Gunther,
who under the Nazi regime is Professor of Anthropology
at the University of Jena, believes that Nordics were
among the ancestors of the Japanese, and Dr. Alfred
Rosenberg, "inspector-general of Nazi mental training,"
laid down, as a teaching officially sanctioned in German
schools, that the biological guarantee of Germany's
leadership is shared by the Japanese. No travesty of
anthropomorphic facts is too startling for propaganda
to announce if the propaganda is backed by force of
arms and concentration camps.

Racialism has become involved in scientific absurdities
under the Third Reich, and it is obviously only a front
used to justify negotiations and persecutions of the
moment. No one knows how long the German-Japanese
alliance will endure. Therefore no one can say what
racist theories will be current in Germany within the
next few years. If the future of racism is like its past,
these theories will depend not on any scientific facts but
on what treaties are signed or not signed and on what
power politics are in the ascendant.

Wherever we study racism, not only in the Third

F I

Reich, there are similar evidences that racist doctrines are invoked for political ends. Nations are hailed now as blood brother, now as destined foe, according to political alignments in peace and in war. In a world as yet unthreatened by the First World War, Carlyle and the historian J. R. Green accounted the valiant Germanic tribes as the ancestors of the English; in 1914 "the Germans," according to English pronouncements, "were what they were fifteen centuries ago, the barbarians who raided our ancestors and destroyed the civilization of the Roman Empire." They became "the Huns," the Mongols from the barbarous East. Russia was on the side of the Allies and racism therefore did obeisance to the affinities of the Celtic soul and the Slavic soul.

The history of national racism, wherever one looks, is the history of chauvinism. In a world which knew the history of Western civilization and the facts of race and wished to distinguish jingoism from fact, such racism would fall on deaf ears. Arrogance and panic, however, are eager to satisfy themselves with an easy and comforting oratory, and the oratory has been provided for them. Desperate peoples, too, are satisfied with a victim, and racism, telling them on the one hand that they are the heirs of the ages, has pointed out to them, on the other, a degenerate breed to extirpate. Racism, seen in its perspective of fifty years, has stemmed not from the sciences—which have repudiated it, and which, indeed, racism has constantly distorted in its pronouncements— but from politics.

Racism in its nationalistic phase, therefore, has been a politician's plaything. It has been bandied about by both enemies against each other even when these are, by anthropomorphic measurements, of similar racial composition; it has been used to discover racial brotherhood where the allies concerned are racially distinct. It is a dangerous plaything, a sword which can be turned in any direction to condemn the enemy of the moment. The inescapable conclusion from a consideration of its history is that these racist claims are a front designed to hide self-seeking aggressions and alliances. They are camouflage. For practical guidance in the world of affairs, we should do well therefore to go behind the racists' slogans and look squarely at the conflict they are trying to foment. Conflicts are sometimes justified, and we may perhaps decide the particular conflict is necessary. But we shall not have decided the matter on the dubious grounds of racism.

WHAT THEY SAY

[Before the French Revolution], however much men of different races may have striven with one another, it was seldom any sense of racial opposition that caused their strife. They fought for land. They plundered one another. They sought glory by conquest. In none of these cases did the thought of racial distinctions come to the front.

James Bryce, *Race Sentiment as a Factor in History*.
Creighton Lecture. London, 1915, pp. 25, 26.

Racial relations today present more dangerous features in the field of interhuman relations than any other point of conflict. Nowhere are mob passions, prejudices, and fears so easy to evoke and so difficult to check.

H. Kohn, " Race Conflict." *Encyclopædia of the Social Sciences*, Vol. XIII, 1934, p. 41.

All reputable anthropologists condemn the malignant nonsense about racial psychology which is preached and published by those who try to justify the oppression of ethnic minorities. Political theories about race are nothing more than instruments of propaganda, devised for the child minds of totalitarian populations.

> E. A. Hooton, *Twilight of Man.* New York, G. P.
> Putnam's Sons, 1939, p. 129.

[Racism] is a method of bolstering up self-esteem and lust for power by means of beliefs which have nothing in their favour except that they are flattering.

> Bertrand Russell, " The Ancestry of Fascism," in *In
> Praise of Idleness.* London, Allen & Unwin, 1935,
> p. 114.

At the best, however, belief in race dogma is just the same as national chauvinism, a symptom of immaturity, lack of experience, and in general of an intellectually poor individuality.

> Friedrich Hertz, *Race and Civilization.* Translated by
> A. S. Levetus and W. Entz. London, Kegan Paul,
> 1928, p. 323.

EIGHT

Why Then Race Prejudice?

As we have seen, all scientific knowledge of race contradicts the idea that human progress has been the work of one race alone or can safely be entrusted to a programme of racial hygiene in the future. No great civilization has been the work of a pure race, and neither history nor psychology, biology nor anthropology can render decisions about the future destiny of any present human breed. Racism has been a travesty of scientific knowledge and has served consistently as special pleading for the supremacy of any group, either class or nation, to which the pleader himself belonged and in whose permanent place in the sun he desired to believe.

Why then does racism have such social importance in our times? No discussion of race and racism can be complete without raising this problem; it is the really burning question, for upon our answer depend the measures we can trust to bring about a cure.

In answering this question we do not need to depend on fine-spun theories of self-communings; history has given the answers many times. We need only to obtain a little perspective. We have seen that racist dogmas as they are stated today are modern. But they express an old human obsession and only the "reasons why" have been altered. This old human obsession is that my group is uniquely valuable, and if it is weakened all valuable things will perish. It were better therefore that a million perish than that one jot or tittle of that unique value should be lost. It becomes my divine mission to extirpate the challenger in whatever field.

The fields change, however. When one field has been won and tolerance and co-operativeness established in what was before an armed camp, we look back upon the episode as an example of human aberration. We think we are different and feel that progress has really been achieved—until other generations arise to look back upon us and decide that we have only shifted mutual intolerance to another area of life. For centuries the battlefield was religion. The Inquisition was not pure barbarism; it was the claim to unique value worked out with all its implications in a field where today we are willing to follow the precept of live and let live. We cannot see racism in perspective without reviewing the occasions and consequences of this earlier arrogance. The fact that it is in the field of religion instead of in the field of race is a reflection of the times; from every other point of view religious persecutions and racial persecutions duplicate one another. Their proponents claimed similar sacred missions; they killed and looted and temporarily enriched themselves. From the standpoint of history both set up false fronts that served political purposes; they destroyed brilliant civilizations. In that one matter in which they differ, religion as over against race, the earlier persecution was at least as justified as the latter. The mediaeval world, convinced that man's existence was an infinitesimal episode in his everlasting life, thought it was common humanity to kill the Antichrist that would lead thousands of souls to damnation. Today we judge this a fallacy, but we must not underestimate the worthy motives of those who believed that they alone had received the divine command; they were not actuated solely by arrogance but by their duty to keep the world faithful to the word of God and to ensure salvation to as many souls as possible. In many churchmen this must have been a worthy emotion, just as today we recognize that patriotism or pride of class is a worthy emotion. However, the judgment of history is that, when either of these worthy emotions is carried into a campaign of extermination of all who belong in other camps, the exterminators suffer with the exterminated and the result is social tragedy.

It was so in the Inquisition. Between 1200 and 1250 the Roman Church was at the apex of its political and temporal power, and these were the great years of the Inquisition. Heresy-hunting was, like Jew-baiting in this decade in Germany, an eruption of minority persecution. It held out the same short-range advantages to the persecutors; it could be used as a front for political purposes; the confiscation of the victims' property enriched the persecutors; and the campaign of hate distracted attention from real issues. The real issues, as they appear in the perspective of history, were two: the first was the issue of freedom of conscience, a freedom which all the tortures of the Inquisition were powerless to uproot and which eventually triumphed in spite of bishops and of kings; the second was the worldliness, and in some cases the corruption, of the Catholic clergy of the period. Even in the highest Council of the Church itself this had been for some time a grave issue, and under Hildebrand (Gregory the Great) and the monk Bernard of Clairvaux there had been valiant efforts toward reform. The times, however, were not auspicious, and the heretics took up the cry of licentiousness against the Church. In stamping out the heretics, the Church embarked upon a campaign of extirpation that absorbed the attention of the faithful and postponed reform in its own ranks.

As a front for political purposes the Inquisition was used in southern France to break the opposition to the growing power of the Capetian kings, and in Florence

its terrible severities under Fra Ruggieri crushed also the
Ghibelline revolt. Wherever the Inquisition flourished—
in France, in Italy, and in Spain—it made common
cause with power politics. The full extent of this common
cause depended upon the practice of confiscating the
heretics' property. The Inquisition is linked in popular
thought with the burning of heretics and the use of torture
to obtain confessions, but the confiscation of property
was sociologically more important. Originally such
property confiscated by the Inquisition belonged not to
the Church but to kings and secular rulers; the right of
the Papacy, and hence of the Inquisitors, to a share of
these riches was not accepted until almost 1250, and
the lion's share went always to secular authorities.
Heresy-hunting was profitable, and all those who sought
riches and power eagerly took advantage of the opportunity, masking their satisfactions behind the dogma
that the heretics were guilty of treason against the
Almighty.

The most celebrated campaign of the Inquisition "in
the name of God" was against the heretics of southern
France in the first half of the thirteenth century. These
heretics were known as the Albigenses and their home
in Provence was a region on which the Roman Church
had a comparatively slight hold. In those days Provence
had little in common with northern France, and her
barons were not vassals of the French king. The house
of Toulouse in southern France had had an especially
brilliant history. For two centuries its court had been
famous for its love of art and literature, for its wealth and
gallantry, and it had established its sovereignty throughout half of Provence. Its cities were the most wealthy
and independent in all of France, and their culture was
greatly influenced by interchange of goods and ideas
with the Saracens of Palestine and the Moors of Spain—

cultures in many ways more enlightened than any others in the Western World at that time.

The heresy of the Albigenses was one of the many mediaeval cults of Manichaeism which taught the strictest asceticism in order that man might free himself from original evil. Manichaean cosmology was an all-embracing dualism of good and evil, of light and darkness, and only by eating the light contained in plants and by eschewing the darkness in meat, only by eliminating the darkness of sensual acts, could righteousness be achieved. "Finished" ascetics, as in many Oriental religions, became divinities and objects of worship to the laity. The dualism of these heresies was simple to grasp and offered an explanation of the evils of the world which had a strong appeal in those troubled times. But we know little of the teachings of the Albigensian sect; most of our knowledge is of their protest against the corruption of the contemporary clergy of the Church. Though Provence lay between great Catholic strongholds to the south and to the north, within its territories the Church was weak; the roots of Provençal culture were not in Rome. The rising burgher class in the towns especially espoused the heresy, and the growing independence of this class made the threat increasingly serious to the Church, which was then at the height of its temporal power. The Papacy ordered the faithful clergy of northern France to preach a campaign of extermination against heretical Provence, and the crusade became one of the most implacable of religious wars. Its conclusion established the Capetian kings of northern France as monarchs in Provence after mass executions had decimated the independent burghers of the cities and had destroyed the civilization that had flourished in southern France. The burning of heretics continued for a hundred years, and at last the cult was exterminated.

The Inquisition did not survive into the modern period, but religious persecution did. One of the longest and most disastrous of these conflicts occurred in sixteenth- and seventeenth-century France. French Protestants of that time were called Huguenots; by the middle of the sixteenth century they had grown greatly in numbers. Like the Albigensian heretics, they were mainly prosperous bourgeois, and the bourgeois of the sixteenth century were opposed to concentration of power in the hands of the French kings. The bloody wars of a generation (1562-1593) were fought in the name of religion, but they masked a conflict which was in great part economic and political. When the Huguenots finally succeeded in having their leader crowned king of France as Henry IV in 1598, the Edict of Nantes proclaimed full civil rights for the Protestants without withdrawing these from the Catholics. It was a signal victory. The law of the land now guaranteed religious and political freedom, but, as has happened before and since that time, the conflict continued. The Crown was Catholic and the Catholic clergy never accepted the Edict of Nantes. Cardinal Richelieu was the greatest power in France; he was both Cardinal and member of the royal council. His domestic policy was to concentrate power in the hands of the king, and to this the Huguenots were opposed. Therefore his internal policy was dominated by his ruthless opposition to the Huguenots, whom he could persecute in the name of religion. Louis XIV, after the death of Richelieu, exercised these royal powers to the full; his dream of absolute monarchy could be realized only if the Huguenots were removed. He carried on a legal persecution, discriminating against them in the exercise of their religion and their civil rights, and the terrible *dragonnades* used torture to compel their acceptance of the "king's religion." It was then, in

1685, that Louis XIV revoked the Edict of Nantes, declaring it was now unnecessary since all his subjects were Catholics. The Protestants emigrated or were sent to the galleys. His act left Louis absolute monarch and enriched his coffers with the expropriated wealth of the Huguenots. It also bled France of more than 400,000 of its inhabitants, intelligent and courageous people who enriched with their abilities the countries which received them.

The Albigensian crusade and the expulsion of the Huguenots are only two high spots in the long story of the suppression of minority groups before the rise of racism.

This suppression of minorities has been continued in the persecutions and nationalistic wars of the twentieth century. In the thirteenth century and in the sixteenth, as in the world today, new economic and social necessities were starting new ferments. Groups arose which opposed some aspect of the old order. The party in power answered by using torment, death, and confiscation of property. Parties in power can always do this, but in the eyes of history these suppressions have purchased an empty triumph. The great period of the Inquisition marked the downward-turning point in the temporal power of the Church no less than the ruin of Provençal civilization, and the Huguenot expulsion gave France only the disastrous and temporary splendour of the reign of Louis XIV. "After me the deluge." Persecution stopped neither the growing demand for freedom of conscience nor the rise of the bourgeoisie.

For a theory of racism there are two conclusions to be drawn from the whole matter. The first is that, in order to understand race persecution, we do not need to investigate race; we need to investigate *persecution*. Persecution was an old, old story before racism was

thought of. Social change is inevitable, and it is always
fought by those whose ties are to the old order. These
ties may be economic or they may be religious, as in
mediaeval Europe, or those of social affiliation, as with
Roman patricians. Those who have these ties will con-
sciously or unconsciously ferret out reasons for believing
that their group is supremely valuable and that the new
claimants threaten the achievements of civilization.
They will raise a cry of rights of inheritance or divine
right of kings or religious orthodoxy or racial purity or
manifest destiny. These cries reflect the temporary conditions of the moment, and all the efforts of the slogan-
makers need not convince us that any one of them is
based on eternal verities. The battle-cries of Nordicism
belong with "Keep Cool with Coolidge" and "He Kept
Us Out of War" of American presidential campaigns,
and with slight changes in social necessities they will be
as evanescent. All slogans are useful in the degree to
which they express the faiths and discontents of the hour.
Religious varieties were politically useful in eras and
regions which had powerful religious interests; when
these were overshadowed by secular privileges and when
cleavages along religious lines became less important,
religious slogans no longer justified the persecution of
minorities as they had in earlier days.

Racial slogans serve the same purpose in the present
century that religious slogans served before—that is, they
are used to justify persecution in the interests of some
class or nation. This racial slogan is peculiarly congenial
to our times. Science is a word to conjure with in this
century; unfortunately it is often used to conjure. It is
not racism alone that has turned to so-called science for
its arguments. A manufacturer of cosmetics conducted
not long ago an investigation of various advertisements
of his wares. He found that the two words which had

most sales-appeal were "immediately" and "scientific."
Every rouge, every face powder must claim a "scientific"
uniqueness, and by this ballyhoo millions are impressed.
It was the same with fake medicines, with drug-store
drinks, and with health foods until it became necessary
to defend the public by federal supervision of manu-
facturers' claims. The slogan of "science" will sell most
things today, and it sells persecution as easily as it sells
rouge. The scientist repeatedly points out that the
advertised rouge is indistinguishable from others, or even
that he has found it especially harmful in a laboratory
test; he points out that no race has a monopoly of
abilities or of virtues, and that, as science, the racists'
claims have no validity. For the scientist, science is a
body of knowledge; he resents its use as a body of magic.
But he knows that *scientific* is the word our civilization
conjures with—in no matter what cause.

The choice of racial slogans to justify conflict is rooted
in still another manner in the conditions of the modern
age. Racial reasons for persecution are convenient just
because in Western civilization today so many different
breeds live in close contact with one another. The racist
cries are raised not because those who raise them have
any claim to belong to pure races, but because they do
not; in other words, because today several ethnic groups
occupy one city or one state, or states that share in one
civilization are engaged in nationalistic wars. Hence
comes the paradox that has been so often pointed out:
that it is the most mongrel peoples of the world who raise
the war-cry of racial purity. From the point of view of
race, this makes nonsense, but from the point of view of
persecution it is inevitable. No group raises battle-cries
against people whose existence is of no moment to it; for
conflict to arise, there must first be contact. Racial
slogans arose therefore in Europe in class and national

conflicts. The old religious slogans for persecution had lost their hold, and the racists evolved in their stead a bastard version of contemporary science. Racism remains in the eyes of history, however, merely another instance of the persecution of minorities for the advantage of those in power.

Once we have recognized that race conflict is only the justification of the persecution that is popular at the moment, the strangest paradox in all racist theory becomes clear. The racists have over and over again derived race prejudice from a race repulsion instinctive in mankind, and historians and biologists and anthropologists have as repetitiously pointed out that such a theory is impossible in view of the universal mixture of races. "Why, if nature abhors race-crossing, does she do so much of it?"[1] But repulsion to intermarriage accompanies any conflict of two groups, however the groups may be defined. They need not be racial. The patricians of Rome recoiled from marriage with plebeians in the same way, the Catholics of France from marriage with the Huguenots. It is not that man has a set of instincts which make only his own race sexually attractive, but that in-groups are unwilling to give status to the outsider. They do not want to share prerogatives with him. If this in-group is defined racially as Anglo-Saxons have defined it in their contact with native peoples of the world, their desire to maintain the in-group will bring about selective mating in marriage, but it notoriously does not prevent mating outside of marriage. The great numbers of half-castes in India and mulattoes in America are testimony to the fact that the antipathy is not instinctive aversion to members of another race.

Those theorists also who have explained race prejudice

[1] Castle, W. E., " Biological and Social Consequences of Race-Crossing," *American Journal of Physical Anthropology*, Vol. IX, pp. 145-146.

by visible racial differences are similarly confused. They have said that race prejudice is caused by obvious and striking contrasts in face and colour. They are, however, mistaking a momentary feature of persecution for a causal one. There was no differentiating skin colour or nose shape in a Huguenot or in the Albigensian victims of the Inquisition. On the other side of the picture, poverty sets groups as visibly apart as the colour of their hair or the shape of their heads. Groups may be set apart by any number of things besides race—by whether they go to Mass or by whether they drop their *h*'s. Members of a primitive tribe have been known to kill at sight members of a neighbouring tribe of the same race and language because they felt that the way they carried their burden baskets was an insult to human beings. Not the fact of "visibility" of skin colour but the fact that racial characteristics are transmitted over so many generations makes racial prejudice a new problem in the world. A man can stop going to Mass or a Huguenot king take the sacrament because "Paris is worth a Mass," or the heroine of *Pygmalion* learn to enunciate her mother tongue in the Oxford fashion, but too dark a Negro cannot "pass" and not even his children's children may be born light enough to do so. This is a problem of relative permanence of distinctions, not specifically of "visibility." In the long course of history persecution has been now more, now less intense; but these variations do not correlate with the presence or absence of racial visibility.

Mistaken explanations of the nature of race prejudice are of minor importance so long as they are concerned with theoretical points like instinctive antipathies or the rôle of racial visibility. There is a far more important issue. The fact that to understand race conflict we need fundamentally to understand *conflict* and not *race*, means something much more drastic. It means that all the deep-seated causes of conflict in any group or between groups are involved in any outbreak of race prejudice. Race will be cried up today in a situation where formerly religion would have been cried up. If civilized men expect to end prejudice—whether religious or racial— they will have to remedy major social abuses, in no way connected with religion or race, to the common advantage. Whatever reduces conflict, curtails irresponsible power, and allows people to obtain a decent livelihood will reduce race conflict. Nothing less will accomplish the task.

For the friction is not primarily racial. We all know what the galling frictions are in the world today: nation-alistic rivalries, desperate defence of the *status quo* by the haves, desperate attacks by the have-nots, poverty, unemployment, and war. Desperate men easily seize upon some scapegoat to sacrifice to their unhappiness; it is a kind of magic by which they feel for the moment that they have laid the misery that has been tormenting them. In this they are actively encouraged by their rulers and exploiters, who like to see them occupied with this violence, and fear that if it were denied them they might demand something more difficult. So Hitler, when his armament programme cut consumers' goods and increased hours of work and lowered real wages, exhorted the nation in 1938 to believe that Germany's defeat in 1919 had been due to Jewry, and encouraged racial riots. And this served two purposes: it gave an undernourished people an outlet harmless to the government, and it allowed the government treasury to appropriate to itself the wealth of the Jews.

In this sequence of events the Third Reich is but following a long series of precedents in European anti-Semitism. During the Middle Ages persecutions of the

Jews, like all mediaeval persecutions, were religious rather then racial. Intermarriage between Jews and Gentiles was condemned, not as a racist measure, but in the same manner as marriages between Catholics and heretics were condemned. The pogroms of the time of the Crusades were carried out by stay-at-home mobs imitating the Crusaders in avenging the death of Christ; the mobs killed Jews, the Crusaders fought the Arabs and Turks. The link between Jews and Turks was not racial; in the period of the Crusades the two were equated because the first had crucified Christ and the second owned his tomb. Nor were persecutions other than those set in motion by the Crusaders directed toward eliminating a racial breed; apostate Jews purchased safety. A renegade Jew denounced or concealed his religion, not his race. The Popes and rulers favourable to the Jews promulgated laws directing that "they should not be baptized by force, constrained to observe Christian festivals nor to wear badges." Even up to the World War some important racists advocated as the cure for conflict, not extinction of the Jewish race, but a racial merger. This was especially true of the great nationalist historian Treitschke, who was one of Germany's foremost advocates of racist salvation at the turn of this century.

As racist persecutions replaced religious persecutions in Europe, however, the inferiority of the Jew became that of *race*. By the 1880's a tidal wave of pogroms and persecutions swept over large parts of Europe. To the people it everywhere appeared that the bourgeoisie were in the saddle, and the Jews, owing to earlier segregation in city ghettos and to restrictions against land-owning, were all bourgeoisie. They were hated for this reason, and persecution was reinforced by the old tradition of religious animosity against the Jews. Racial anti-Semitism was all too easy to arouse. In Germany in the 'eighties an anti-Semitic demagogue of evil repute was cynically encouraged by members of the Conservative Party in order to strengthen with his following their opposition to the Social Democrats; synagogues were burned and violence against the Jews went unpunished. The charge of Jewish ritual murder was revived. In France, the anti-Semitic movement came to a climax in the 1890's with the famous Dreyfus affair. It marks probably the climax of pre-War anti-Semitism in Europe. The reactionary party was most strongly represented in the Army, and the "framing" of a prominent Jewish staff officer, Captain Alfred Dreyfus, and his conviction of treason on forged evidence, were the occasion for a year-long conflict that rocked the nation. To the honour of France, the plot was laid bare, Dreyfus was exonerated, and it was shown that those who were really guilty of the treason had attempted to hide themselves behind a Jew because of popular anti-Semitism.

The more closely one studies European anti-Semitism in its modern racial guise, the less it appears that the conflict is racial; it is the old problem of unequal citizen-ship rights. Whenever one group, whether industrial workers or a religious sect or a racial group, is discrimin-ated against before the law or in equal claims to life, liberty, and jobs, there will always be powerful interests to capitalize this fact and to divert violence from those responsible for these conditions into channels where it is relatively safe to allow. In the case of the Jews we inherit from the old era of religious persecution all the necessary shibboleths of hate, and these are easily turned to account in a new setting. In addition there is excep-tional profit; unlike most discriminated-against minor-ities, the Jews often provide rich contraband and are therefore marked objects for persecution to a poverty-stricken government or populace.

The cure for anti-Semitism, therefore, logically lies, as in all minority conflicts, in the extension to all men of full citizenship rights and of full opportunity to make good in any field. There would have been no Dreyfus case if certain traitors had not felt that a framed Jew would be found guilty by the courts. There would have been no nation-wide pogroms in Germany in 1938 if al' those who took part in them had known the state would hold them accountable. It is not only for the sake of the persecuted that the full rights of minorities need to be maintained. The minorities may be only martyrs, but the persecutors revert to savagery. If we are unwilling or unable to pay the price of equality in human rights, we, the persecutors, suffer brutalization in ourselves whenever we fall into the trap set for us.

The case of the Negro since the Civil War in America points the same social lesson. The only trustworthy objective in any colour-line programme is the ultimate elimination of legal, educational, economic, and social discriminations. The fact that such elimination is not accepted even as an ultimate objective in most parts of the South is due to the persistence of slave-owner attitudes on the one hand and, on the other, to the degrading conditions under which great numbers of Negroes have lived in the United States. Granted that great numbers of Negroes are not ready for full citizenship, the social conditions which perpetuate their poverty and ignorance must be remedied before anyone can judge what kind of citizens they might be in other, more favourable circumstances. To be able to live a decent life and be respected for it, without being subjected to a blanket damnation that one's personal life cannot remove, is a human right, the granting of which would have immense social repercussions.

In periods and places where social institutions have

made this possible for the Negro in the New World, the results have been incomparably better than those in the United States since the Civil War. Lord Bryce, an excellent observer, said of Brazil: "Brazil is the one country in the world, besides the Portuguese colonies on the east and west coasts of Africa, in which a fusion of the European and African races is proceeding unchecked by law or custom. The doctrines of human equality and human solidarity have here their perfect work. The work is so far satisfactory that there is little or no class friction. The white man does not lynch or maltreat the Negro; indeed I have never heard of a lynching anywhere in South America except occasionally as part of a political convulsion. The Negro is not accused of insolence and does not seem to develop any more criminality than naturally belongs to any ignorant population with loose notions of morality and property. What ultimate effect the intermixture of blood will have on the European element in Brazil I will not venture to predict. If one may judge from a few remarkable cases it will not necessarily reduce the intellectual standard." [1]

Such conditions were possible in Brazil only because of the extreme lack of racial discrimination which the Portuguese everywhere showed in their post-Columbian colonization; with the growing influence of non-Portuguese cultures in modern Brazil, the Negro has to some extent suffered. With growing discrimination against his race, the usual effects have followed, small though these consequences are in Brazil in comparison with the United States. But while discrimination was at a minimum, the social results were good.

To minimize racial persecution, therefore, it is necessary to minimize conditions which lead to persecution;

[1] Bryce, James, *South America, Observations and Impressions*. London, Macmillan & Co., 1912, pp. 477, 480.

it is not necessary to minimize race. Race is not in itself the source of the conflict. Conflict arises whenever any group—in this case, a race—is forged into a class by discriminations practised against it; the race then becomes a minority which is denied rights to protection before the law, rights to livelihood and to participation in the common life. The social problem does not differ whether such a group is racially distinguished or whether it is not; in either case the healthy social objective is to do away with minority discriminations.

We are so far from doing this in the modern world that it is likely to seem a programme impossible of achievement. Even so, this is not the total programme for a world free of race conflict. It is not enough merely to legislate human rights for the minorities. The majorities, also—the persecutors—must have solid basis for confidence in their own opportunity to live in security and decency. Otherwise, whatever the laws, whatever the guarantees, they will find out a victim and sacrifice him as a scapegoat to their despair. Everything that is done in any nation to eliminate unemployment, to raise the standard of living, to ensure civil liberties, is a step in the elimination of race conflict. Whatever is done to fasten fear upon the people of a nation, to humiliate individuals, to abrogate civil liberties, to deny coveted opportunities, breeds increased conflict. Men have not, for all their progress in civilization, outgrown the hen-yard; a hen who is pecked at by a cock attacks, not the cock, but a weaker hen; this weaker hen attacks a still weaker, and so on down to the last chicken. Man, too, has his "pecking order," and those who have been victims, even though they belong to the "superior race," will require victims.

The truth of the matter is that these two aspects of a programme for preventing the ravages of racism—democratic opportunity for the privileged and for the under-privileged—cannot be separated from one another: they are web and woof. One of the great political advantages of racist slogans is that the under-privileged may use them. Therefore the unemployed and the low-income groups can vent, through this alleged racist "superiority," the hatred that is engendered by their fear and insecurity. Studies in America have many times shown that anti-Semitism is strongest among low-income groups and that the high peaks of racial per-secution have coincided with the low troughs of depression periods. While America raises Negro standards of living, of health, and of education in the South, therefore, it is necessary also to raise the standards of the Southern poor Whites. Until we have "made democracy work" so that the nation's full man-power is drafted for its common benefit, racist persecution will continue in America. Until housing and conditions of labour are raised above the needlessly low standards which prevail in many sections of the country, scapegoats of some sort will be sacrificed to poverty. Until the regulation of industry has enforced the practice of social responsibility, there will be exploitation of the most helpless racial groups, and this will be justified by racist denunciations.

Hard-boiled economists and statesmen recognize today the short-sightedness of policies which allow such con-ditions to continue and to become intensified. Those who fight to perpetuate them are repeating the errors of the Albigensian crusade and the Huguenot expulsion; they are gaining a false and temporary advantage at the expense of their own permanent welfare. National pros-perity, however thin you cut it, has two surfaces: ability to sell means ability to buy; employment means pro-duction. Whatever groups battle with each other, under conditions of modern industry and finance, the most important condition of either one's getting more is that the other shall also get more. Since their conflict is truly suicidal, it is necessary for the benefit of the contestants themselves that far-sighted regulations should be imposed on both parties.

In the last decade we have grown to recognize much more fully the responsibility that rests on the state for achieving satisfactory national conditions, and from the standpoint of history it is likely that this rôle of the state will in the long run be extended rather than curtailed. A democratic state, when it lives up to its minimum definition at all, is the one institution which represents all the parts of the body politic. It can propose for itself programmes which will eventually benefit the whole body. It is hard to see how this responsibility for the whole can be taken today except by the national government, and in the past decade state regulation has increased, national treasuries all over the Western World have been opened for the relief of the unemployed, and compulsory old-age insurance is in operation in many nations. These and other national undertakings can be used to minimize economic discrimination. Equality in the matter of civil liberties is closely bound up with such programmes, and so long as civil liberties are made more, rather than less, equal for different groups, there is no historical reason for fearing the increased rôle of the state. For the true goal in any programme for a better America is that all men may be able to live so that self-respect is possible and so that they may have confidence that prosperity will spread its benefits widely over the population.

The cultural anthropologist has the best reason in the world to know that conflict is eliminated only as men work together for common benefits and obtain them in common. In most of the tribes the anthropologist knows, he can study side by side two different codes of ethics: one is that of open-handed hospitality and liberality and sharing, along with condemnation of aggressions like stealing and murder; the other is death at sight, torture, and the exaltation of robbery. The first code a man applies to those whose economic and social activities benefit him; these form an in-group within which none but moral reprobates are penalized. No matter who is successful in the hunt, the whole in-group benefits; any special skills any man may possess are an asset to the group as a whole. The priests conduct ceremonies for the good of the tribe and for common advantages like increase of plants and animals; warriors defend the little group against predatory outsiders. The second code a man applies to tribes with whom his tribe makes no common cause. No activities of theirs feed or house or bless or defend him. They are outside the pale. It is only a question of whether he kills his enemies first or they kill him.

The in-group code of ethics arises, however, only as the institutions of a society provide for shared advantages. When increase of food supply is not a common benefit, but something one man must get at the expense of another; when supernatural power is not used for general blessings, like rain, which falls on all, but for charms to use for personal ends against a neighbour; when legal or economic or political institutions put one man at the mercy of his neighbours, persecution develops. The gain or loss of all men is no longer my own gain or loss, and the tribe is no longer a unit within which in-group ethics operate. The persecution that develops is most often sorcery. Sorcery is a very evil thing, and when society does not officially punish it the victim has no redress. Unchecked sorcery societies are like modern nations with Ogpus and Gestapos, and they act out in deeds Hitler's dictum: "We need hatred, hatred, and then more hatred."

In-group ethics is therefore a reflection of the fact that all members share in their tribal enterprises and do actually profit from one another's activities. In-group mutual support is as native to the human race as out-group hostility; it is not something precarious and achieved only by isolated individuals at the end of a long social evolution. It arose long before the higher ethical religions with their teachings of altruism and duty. It occurs automatically whenever the social order makes it advantageous. It is at home among the lowest savages, and the one essential contribution modern civilization has made has been to enlarge the size of the in-group. In this there has been incomparable progress. Millions today recognize their common cause as citizens of a great nation, or as members of a party, or as financiers, or as workers, whereas in past history some little territory might be divided into a dozen hostile groups recognizing no common bonds. Today the increasing complexity of the processes of production, the ease of transportation, the interdependence of financial systems have brought it about that people in the remotest part of civilization suffer from catastrophe in another part.

The very progress of civilization, therefore, has laid the foundation for a vast extension of in-group mutual dependency and mutual support. Mankind has not yet adjusted its institutions to the real requirements of the world it has created, and this cultural lag today threatens the very bases of international life. Many serious students of human affairs have been driven to despair. The world of our fathers, they conclude, has been destroyed because it tried to ignore the real facts of human nature; it tried to impose a peaceful social order on a predatory animal. The lesson we should learn from

G

recent events, they say, is that man is by nature a beast of prey who will always tear and rend his weaker neighbours; we must recognize that wars and racial persecutions are inevitable in human destiny. To the anthropologist such a counsel of despair is demonstrably false. In-group ethics are as "innate" as out-group ethics, *but they occur only when certain social conditions are fulfilled.* We cannot get in-group ethics without meeting those conditions. In our own country this means that a better America will be one which benefits not some groups alone but all citizens; so long as there is starvation and joblessness in the midst of abundance we are inviting the deluge. To avert it, we must "strongly resolve" that all men shall have the basic opportunity to work and to earn a living wage, that education and health and decent shelter shall be available to all, that, regardless of race, creed, or colour, civil liberties shall be protected.

The elimination of race conflict is a task of social engineering. But what of education? It is often said that our school systems must make themselves responsible for ending race prejudice, and attempts have been made to achieve tolerance by special instruction. This is of great importance, but we should be quite clear about the limits of its effectiveness; otherwise, in the end we shall cry that we were betrayed because it has not succeeded. All education, whether of children or of adults, is important and necessary because it makes for an enlightened mind and for unbiased impulses. These are essential because without them discriminations may not be done away with at all and barriers to opportunity may never be thrown down. But good impulses are socially effective only when they have accomplished these results. "Hell is paved with good intentions"—intentions which were blindly regarded as ends in themselves and not as mere preliminaries. This is a platitude, but one which is often forgotten in discussions of the rôle of our schools in racial matters. If we are to make good use of the great powers of education in combating racism, two goals should be kept clearly distinct. On the one hand, it is desirable to teach in the regular social studies the facts of race and of the share of different races in our civilization. On the other hand, it is necessary to hold up ideals of a functioning democracy; it is necessary to help children to understand the mutual interdependence of different groups; it is necessary to encourage comparison of our social conditions with conditions which are better than ours as well as with those that are worse. It is necessary that they should be taught to think of unsatisfactory conditions not as inescapable facts of nature, but as ones which with effort can be done away with. Only through such education can school instruction lay the basis for the amelioration of race conflict. We cannot trust to teaching them about the glories of Chinese civilization or the scientific achievements of the Jews. That is worth doing, but if we leave it at that and expect them to become racially tolerant we have deceived ourselves. The fatal flaw in most arguments which would leave to the schools the elimination of race conflict is that they propose education *instead of* social engineering. Nothing but hypocrisy can come of such a programme.

The programme that will avail against racism is called today "making democracy work." In so far as it is achieved in America it will produce the kind of behaviour it has always produced in a mutually supporting ingroup. Change, we must recognize, is always difficult and produces dislocations. But if we know the direction in which we must move, we can resolve to pay the necessary costs of change. The Arabians have a proverb: "'What will you have?' said the Prophet, 'take it and pay for it.'" We must pay for a democracy that works, but fortunately in this case we can reassure ourselves with the knowledge that, even in financial accounting, government investment in rehousing and rebuilding America, in soil conservation, in health and education, and in increasing the nation's purchasing power through insurance benefits, pay their own way with handsome returns. A price is exacted also for a social order like Nazi Germany, and that price, in lowered standards of living, in brutalization, in denial of human rights, in sabotage of science and the intellectual life, is higher than any costs of democracy. In persecuting victims, the Nazis were themselves victimized.

Our Founding Fathers believed that a nation could be administered without creating victims. It is for us to prove that they were not mistaken.

WHAT THEY SAY

In the gain or loss of one race all the rest have equal share.

James Russell Lowell in *The Crisis*.

There is no irrepressible conflict between Oriental and Western civilizations. On the contrary, they are complementary to each other, not necessarily competitive.

Paul Samuel Reinsch, *Intellectual and Political Currents in the Far East*. London, Constable & Co., 1911, p. 35.

Every effort of the Negro to move, to raise and improve his social status, rather than his condition, has invariably met with opposition, aroused prejudice, and stimulated racial animosities. Race prejudice, so conceived, is merely an elementary expression of conservatism.

R. E. Park, " Bases of Race Prejudice," *Annals of the American Academy*, Vol. CXL, Nov. 1928, p. 13.

Race thus has a profound social significance. . . . It is made the symbol of cultural status and thus serves to justify the exploitation of the weaker group with the inevitable political and cultural consequences. Being a symbol of cultural status it serves automatically to classify individuals, and so to retard their advance by limiting their freedom and determining the cultural values to which they have access.

> E. B. Reuter, *American Race Problem.* New York, T. Y. Crowell Co., 1927, p. 34.

The philosophical implication of race-thinking is that by offering us the mystery of heredity as an explanation, it diverts our attention from the social and intellectual factors that make up personality.

> Jacques Barzun, *Race: a Study in Modern Superstition.* London, Methuen & Co., 1938, p. 282.

For the combating of racism before it sinks its ugly fangs deep in our body politic, the scientist has a special responsibility. Only he can clean out the falsities which have been masquerading under the name of science in our colleges, our high schools, and our public prints. Only he can show how groundless are the claims that one race, one nation, or one class has any God-given right to rule.

> Henry A. Wallace, U.S. Secretary of Agriculture, in an address delivered at the World's Fair, New York, October 14, 1939.

Anti-alien campaigns of whatever nature are a sickening travesty of Americanism. We can contribute nothing of more value to a sick world than proof that men and women of different racial origins can get along together peaceably and democratically. Go far enough back and we are all aliens.

> *New York Times,* Editorial, December 7, 1939.

Resolutions and Manifestoes of Scientists

RESOLUTION OF
THE AMERICAN ASSOCIATION OF UNIVERSITY PROFESSORS
(Passed unanimously, December 28, 1938)

BE IT RESOLVED: that the American Association of University Professors at its annual meeting of 1938, believing that the primary duty of the college and university is the search for and diffusion of truth, express its abhorrence at the action of totalitarian regimes which prevent the accomplishment of this duty by persecuting teachers on account of their race, religion, or political ideals; and that it express its sympathetic approval of its colleagues living under such regimes who, even in apparent silence, are protesting against the action of their governments.

RESOLUTION OF
THE AMERICAN ANTHROPOLOGICAL ASSOCIATION
(December 1938) [1]

Whereas, The prime requisites of science are the honest and unbiased search for truth and the freedom to proclaim such truth when discovered and known; and,

Whereas, Anthropology in many countries is being conscripted and its data distorted and misinterpreted to serve the cause of an unscientific racialism rather than the cause of truth;

[1] *Science,* Vol. 89, No. 2298, January 13, 1939.

Be it resolved, That the American Anthropological Association repudiates such racialism and adheres to the following statement of facts:

(1) Race involves the inheritance of similar physical variations by large groups of mankind, but its psychological and cultural connotations, if they exist, have not been ascertained by science.

(2) The terms "Aryan" and "Semitic" have no racial significance whatsoever. They simply denote linguistic families.

(3) Anthropology provides no scientific basis for discrimination against any people on the ground of racial inferiority, religious affiliation, or linguistic heritage.

PSYCHOLOGISTS' STATEMENT (EXCERPTS) AT
THE ANNUAL MEETING OF THE AMERICAN PSYCHO-
LOGICAL ASSOCIATION
(December 1938) [1]

THE current emphasis upon "racial differences" in Germany and Italy, and the indications that such an emphasis may be on the increase in the United States and elsewhere, make it important to know what psychologists and other social scientists have to say in this connection.

In the experiments which psychologists have made upon different peoples, no characteristic inherent psychological differences which fundamentally distinguish so-called "races" have been disclosed. This statement is supported by the careful surveys of these experiments in such books as *Race Psychology* by Professor T. R. Garth

[1] A statement prepared by the Executive Council of the *Society for the Psychological Study of Social Issues*, representing an organization of more than 400 professional psychologists.

of the University of Denver, *Individual Differences* by
Professor Frank S. Freeman of Cornell University, *Race
Differences* by Professor Otto Klineberg of Columbia
University, and *Differential Psychology* by Dr. Anne
Anastasi of Barnard College. There is no evidence for
the existence of an inborn Jewish or German or Italian
mentality. Furthermore, there is no indication that the
members of any group are rendered incapable by their
biological heredity of completely acquiring the culture
of the community in which they live. This is true not
only of the Jews in Germany, but also of groups that
actually are physically different from one another. The
Nazi theory that people must be related by blood in
order to participate in the same cultural or intellectual heritage has absolutely no support from scientific
findings.

Psychologists look elsewhere for the explanation of
current racial hatred and persecution. It is certain that
the Nazi race theories have been developed not on the
basis of objective fact, but under the domination of
powerful emotional attitudes. A well-known psychological tendency leads people to blame others for their
own misfortunes, and the Nazis have found in the Jew
a convenient psychological scapegoat for their own
economic and political disabilities. In certain Czecho-
slovakian localities as well, Jews are now being blamed
for the dismemberment of the country. There can be
no doubt that economic factors are also directly involved,
as the recent enormous levy on Jewish capital in Germany
has amply demonstrated. Theories of Jewish plots and
machinations are an excuse, a rationalization, for the
expropriation of badly needed property. This attitude
is not new, nor is it restricted to Central Europe.

Racial and national attitudes are psychologically
complex, and cannot be understood except in terms of

their economic, political, and historical backgrounds. Psychologists find no basis for the explanation of such attitudes in terms of innate mental differences between racial and national groups. The many attempts to establish such differences have so far met with failure. Even if successful they would offer no justification for repressive treatment of the type now current in Germany. In the scientific investigations of human groups by psychologists, no conclusive evidence has been found for racial or national differences in native intelligence and inherited personality characteristics. Certainly no individual should be treated as an inferior merely because of his membership in one human group rather than another. Here in America we have clear indications of the manner in which members of different racial and national groups have combined to create a common culture.

Council Members

F. H. ALLPORT, Syracuse University.

GORDON ALLPORT, Harvard University.

J. F. BROWN, Kansas University.

HADLEY CANTRIL, Princeton University.

L. W. DOOB, Yale University.

H. B. ENGLISH, Ohio State University.

FRANKLIN FEARING, University of California, Los Angeles.

GEORGE W. HARTMANN, Columbia University.

I. KRECHEVSKY, University of Colorado.

GARDNER MURPHY, Columbia University.

T. C. SCHNEIRLA, New York University.

E. C. TOLMAN, University of California.

BIOLOGISTS' MANIFESTO (EXCERPTS) AT
THE SEVENTH INTERNATIONAL GENETICS CONGRESS,
EDINBURGH

(August 28-30, 1939) [1]

THE question "how could the world's population be
improved most effectively genetically" raises far broader
problems than the purely biological ones, problems
which the biologist unavoidably encounters as soon as
he tries to get the principles of his own special field put
into practice. For the effective genetic improvement of
mankind is dependent upon major changes in social
conditions and correlative changes in human attitudes.
In the first place, there can be no valid basis for estimating
and comparing the intrinsic worth of different individuals
without economic and social conditions which provide
approximately equal opportunities for all members of
society instead of stratifying them from birth into classes
with widely different privileges.

The second major hindrance to genetic improvement
lies in the economic and political conditions which foster
antagonism between different peoples, nations, and
"races." The removal of race prejudices and of the
unscientific doctrine that good or bad genes are the
monopoly of particular peoples or of persons with features
of a given kind will not be possible, however, before the
conditions which make for war and economic exploitation have been eliminated. This requires some effective
sort of federation of the whole world, based on the
common interests of all its peoples.

Thirdly, it cannot be expected that the raising of
children will be influenced actively by considerations of
the worth of future generations unless parents in general

have a very considerable economic security, and unless they are extended such adequate economic, medical, educational, and other aids in the bearing and rearing of each additional child that the having of more children does not overburden either of them. As the woman is more especially affected by child-bearing and rearing she must be given special protection to ensure that her reproductive duties do not interfere too greatly with her opportunities to participate in the life and work of the community at large. These objects cannot be achieved unless there is an organization of production primarily for the benefit of consumer and worker, unless the conditions of employment are adapted to the needs of parents and especially of mothers, and unless dwellings, towns, and community services generally are reshaped with the good of children as one of their main objectives. . . .

The day when economic reconstruction will reach the stage where such human forces will be released is not yet, but it is the task of this generation to prepare for it, and all steps along the way will represent a gain, not only for the possibilities of the ultimate genetic improvement of man, to a degree seldom dreamed of hitherto, but at the same time, more directly, for human mastery over those more immediate evils which are so threatening our modern civilization.

(*Original Signers*)

F. A. E. CREW, F.R.S.	J. S. HUXLEY, F.R.S.
J. B. S. HALDANE, F.R.S.	H. J. MULLER.
S. C. HARLAND.	J. NEEDHAM.
L. T. HOGBEN, F.R.S.	

Index